THOSE PASSED BY

Nicaragua
Those Passed By

Vern Asleson

2010
Galde Press
Lakeville, Minnesota, U.S.A.

Nicaragua: Those Passed By
© Copyright 2008 by Vern Asleson
All rights reserved.
Printed in the United States of America

Second Edition
Second Printing, 2010

Cover design by Christopher Wells and Andrew Wood
The cover depicts a boy at the Guasimo refugee camp, Jacaleapa, El Paraiso,
Honduras. Though most likely with his mother, where might his father be? In
prison under the Sandinistas, with the Contras, in the refugee camp, or killed?

Library of Congress Cataloging-in-Publication Data

Asleson, Vern
  Nicaragua : those passed by / Vern Asleson.—1st ed.
     p. cm.
  Includes bibliographical references and index.
  ISBN 1-931942-16-1 (trade pbk.)
  1. Nicaragua—Politics and government—1979-1990.
  2. Terrorism—Nicaragua—History—20th century. 3. Nicaragua—Social
  conditions. 4. Nicaragua—Economic conditions. 5. Interviews—Nicaragua.
  I. Title.
  F1528.A82 2004
  972.8505'3—dc22

                                                    2004007363

Galde Press
PO Box 460
Lakeville, Minnesota 55044–0460

Contents

Preface for
Twenty-First-Century Publication

With research basically compiled within the second half of the 1980s and geared to its 1986-87 historical interviews, *Nicaragua: Those Passed By* should be granted prudent circumspection from those observing present realities and who hold the future in mind. This overview should take on added importance since the Leftist party featured in the following accounts were in year 2000 making a very sinister and significant twenty-first-century return to political power, all due to a dearth of morality and ignorance of omnipresent citizenry who choose to be guided by clever liars.

For a dramatic viewing into the not too distant past, this book contains on-the-spot snapshots of what took place in people's lives when the Left took control of a country not all that far from the southern border of Texas. At that time, this was not recognized as unusual because of Liberal media bias and unwillingness to point out political realities, seconded by Congressional leaders whose dishonesty and ineptness could be hidden.

Let us allow the residents from western Nicaragua to elucidate their experiences of an awful political takeover in Book One.

Book Two elaborates on the tragic drama, mainly from the eyes of two national, racial minorities.

The ensuing material should aid one in understanding why there could have been such a thing as an "Iran-Contra" controversy. One might focus on the real "bad guys" who forced heroes to do what heroes had to do and made these heroes the "fall guys" for the mockery of what a good North American neighbor should have been.

Acknowledgments

My thanks to John and Nana Gill who made it possible for me to conduct interviews in Honduras and in further assistance composing this work.

Greatly appreciated, also, were the many who aided in multitudinous ways. To name a few: those who extended personal assistance while in Honduras, notably, Bill Stewart and Carmen Winkler; those who did translation chores, Suyapa Reina, John Spence and Andrew Swan; special thanks to John Baldwin who piloted so magnificently in a single-engine aircraft while I was in Honduras as well as the outward-bound flight to the U.S.; the constructive suggestions from readers of the manuscript; and the many who prayed for my welfare, the results of which were felt more than once.

Honduras

Nicaragua

Gracias
A Dios

Prumnitara

Puerto Lempira
Kruta River

*Cabo Gracias
a Dios*

Mocoron

Wangklawala Ihaya

Auka

Anris
Kum
Wasla
Saklin
Bilwaskarma

Bismuna

Sandy Bay

Aasang
San
Ramon
Rus Rus
Waspuk
Krasa
Waspam
Leimus
Raiti
San Carlos
La Tranquera

Coco River

Francia Sirpi

Teupasenti

Bocay

Tasba Pry

Tegucigalpa

Bonanza

Sahsa

Krukira
Twapi

Las Trojes
Capire

La Rosita

Danli
Limon

Jalapa
Wamblan
Siuna

JINOTEGA

**ATLANTICO
NORTE**

**Puerto
Cabezas**

Jacaleapa

Karata
Wawa

La Lodosa

La Paz
Murra

Limbaika

Haulover Creek

El Jicaro

**NEUVA
SEGOVIA**

Alamikamba

Wounta
Walpasiksa

Ocotal

Quilali

Prinzapolka
Puerta Isabel

MADRIZ

San Sabastian
de Yali

ESTELÍ

CHINANDEGA

Esteli

MATAGALPA

**Caribbean
Sea**

Karawala

Chinandega

Matagalpa

Corinto

LEON

BOACO

**ATLÁNTICO
SUR**

Tasbapauni

V. Momotombo

Leon

MANAGUA

Kukra Hill

Pearl Lagoon

La Paz
Cento

*Lago de
Managua*

Tipitapa

Rama

Managua

CHONTALIS

Bluefields

Masaya

GRANADA

Granada

Rama Key

Pigeon Key

CARAZO

*Lago
de
Nicaragua*

**RIO
SAN JUAN**

Turswani

**Pacific
Ocean**

Rivas

Archipiélago
de Solentiname

RIVAS

San Carlos

Costa Rica

San Juan River

Introduction

With approximately three million souls remaining in Nicaragua, perhaps twenty percent[1] fled because of the Communist takeover of their land.[2]

Can the reader begin to visualize problems which could arise from such tremendous social upheaval and suffering? Very little of this is reported. Even what has been revealed is usually slanted in favor of the Left or diluted.

Those interviewed in the following pages represent the many more who cannot talk. The valuable qualities they represent may someday be a factor in bringing to judgment the unjust, power-driven Communist leaders ruling their land today.

Too late to rectify a national downfall, Nicaragua fell prey to situations which you will discover in the ensuing accounts of pathos.

Book I

Citizens of Western Nicaragua

Zaida Rodriguez vda de Ortez
Danli, El Paraiso, Honduras
October 8, 1986

"Contra Dogs"

A witness to what was happening in the rural mountainous region of northern Nicaragua, this noble lady paid a lonesome price: the death of her husband. Many should feel encouraged by this small farmer's wife, who did what she could in the global struggle against Communism.

On September 20, 1986, Zaida Rodriguez vda [widowed] de [of] Ortez [husband's family name] fled from Limon, Nueva Segovia, Nicaragua, to Honduras with five of her eight children: two girls, ages fourteen and ten, and three boys, eight, two and one. The three oldest, two girls (twenty and eighteen) and a boy (sixteen), had preceded their mother into exile by two years.

Zaida's husband, Santiago, whose age was the same as hers (forty) had been killed on March 10, 1986, near Limon while fighting on the side of the Freedom Fighters[1] against Sandinista[2] army units which were returning from a major incursion into Honduras[3]. Though fighting friends had buried him along with other fallen compatriots, the grave sites were later exhumed by Sandinista soldiers, who, as they were stripping the slain of clothes and shoes, recognized Santiago. Knowing that he had relatives nearby, they mutilated[4] his remains and informed the family that his body was in the mountains and that dogs were eating the corpse.

After anxiously pleading with the authorities for over three months to be allowed to walk the couple of miles to retrieve the body, Zaida finally was granted permission to search. What she and relatives found was not pleasant. Though she recognized her husband's disfigured and deteriorated body, his head had been severed, never to be found, the torso mutilated and the left leg missing.

For whatever value the information was worth, neighbors informed Zaida that the Sandinistas kept a collection of heads at their military base on the site of the former Somoza[5] farm, La Miya, located near Jalapa, Nueva Segovia.

With Santiago's remains being placed into a plastic bag and buried in a public and not a Catholic cemetery, the question may be asked, "Why was this done, as the family was Roman Catholic?"

The answer is found in the character of the local parish priest, Father Evaristo, who serves the two-point Jalapa-Limon churches and lives in Jalapa. Having fought with the Sandinistas against the former government, he now carries a weapon and calls upon his congregation to take up arms to defend the community against the "Contra dogs."

As there had been no burial Mass, friends and relatives got together with Zaida nine days later and remembered Santiago in an informal way.

A member among the FDN Freedom Fighters for two and half years including the six months which were spent in actual combat before his death, he was known by his pseudonym, Milagro ("miracle"). Joining most others in his community whose sympathies were not with the new government, he refused the state requests that he take up arms against the Contras and did not attend Sandinista Party public meetings. He viewed the present regime's power bloc as criminal in the things which it did to fellow Nicaraguans, with some of the latter being allowed to die at home.

For anyone in his household to be able to walk to and tend the family coffee farm of forty *manzanas* (seventy acres), where there was also a house, an official permit first would have had to be obtained. Even though the family land lay about three miles from Limon, there was also an additional three miles to the Honduran border. Because the authorities were afraid that anyone in his family who might be traveling in the direction of Honduras would also cross the border in order to join the Contra forces, Santiago was not given permission to go to the farm.

Although allowing her children to attend public grade school only in their early years, Zaida took them out as they got older because history classes were geared only for Sandinista politics and their party's propped-up heroes. Addition and subtraction were taught in terms of bullets, rifles, cannons, etc. with the United States as the enemy of the people. Teachers were stressing that there was no God…and that others were not to talk about Him, either.

It was government policy to bother and intimidate faithful Christians during worship services. Evangelical Protestants in her village were examples of this. The military directed rifle fire at sanctuaries, compelling worshippers to evacuate the buildings out of fear for their lives. These intimidated ones then would be informed when they could or could not hold congregational meetings. Because of simulated dangers, they were coerced to conduct scheduled programs at inconvenient hours.

The Catholic church in Limon, on the other hand, was not harassed in this manner for reasons already mentioned. Of course, individual parishioners such as Zaida and her family were carefully watched. They did not fit into the mold on which Communist officials insisted for them.

All community men were forced to take military training from Libyans and Cubans and compelled to do battle against the Freedom Fighters. With their refusal to take up arms, many men were thrown into prison.

Zaida said that she had conversed with young people who had been in great fear for their lives while in the Nicaraguan armed services. Once under military discipline, they were not granted permission to return to their homes. This was done to insure the separation of their moral and spiritual ties.[6]

Because she did not attend CDS[7] meetings, Zaida was treated with disdain and allowed to purchase milk only within the first six months after the birth of her baby boy. She was not issued a ration card. She was permitted to purchase food items only after others in favored status with the local CDS had received what they needed. Although she was aided by friends in securing necessities from time to time, the only choice open to her was to purchase from the more expensive black market.

Zaida emphasized how people had to collaborate with the local CDS or they would have died from hunger. An example of this was the case of tobacco workers, who were compensated with the extremely low wages of

300 *cordobas* per day.[8] The workers were warned that if they failed to attend the July 19, 1986, Seventh Anniversary of the Sandinista Party's takeover of Nicaragua, they would lose their jobs and no food would be sold to them at the lower state prices.

Zaida met, discreetly and from time to time, with a woman whose husband also was a Freedom Fighter, but great care had to be exercised. The authorities had given warning that if anyone allowed a Contra into the village, the whole community would be burned down. When someone knocked at her door at night indicating that he was from the Contras, she did not open the door.

Nevertheless, householders had their doors kicked in and were arrested by officials. Though wives and families might have seen loved ones transported away in military vehicles, inquiry at the nearest military base would very likely be answered with "Maybe the Contras took them?" Many of these widowed wives went to Honduras.

When Zaida left Nicaragua, she had to abandon what the family owned. As all would be confiscated by the Sandinista government, she had no other choice but to live as a stateless refugee in another country.[9]

In the United States, with the Reagan Administration's March 1986 announcement of a Nicaraguan incursion, there developed political wrangling over Contra funding.[10]

Bayardo Antonio Santeliz.

Bayardo Antonio Santeliz

Danli, El Paraiso, Honduras

November 4, 1986

> In the spring of 1985, the author heard a radio report of
> Bayardo's visit to America. The President of the United
> States introduced him as an unnamed Nicaraguan Pente-
> costal pastor whose ear had been lost, an atrocity allegedly
> committed by the Sandinista government. But the infor-
> mation was positioned as not being as reliable as it could
> have been.[1]

7

"Parasites of the Revolution"

Bayardo, a black-haired, twenty-seven year old with a 145-pound, five-foot-nine-inch frame and noticeable facial scars, answered interview questions in a mild manner. His voice was soft, gentle, and endearing.

The tragic crime which happened to Bayardo and his co-workers within a Christian congregation occurred three years after the Sandinistas had taken power. It took place twenty-five air miles north- northwest of Managua in the Department of Leon, approximately twenty miles from the city of Leon, and about twenty-five miles from Mina El Limon where Bayardo had been raised from childhood. This was a coffee-farming community located near the famous Momotombo,[2] one of Nicaragua's best known volcanoes, which extends 4,400 feet to a cone-shaped top overlooking a peninsula at the northwestern section of Lake Managua.

Bayardo was six years old when his father and mother died. Adopted by an elderly couple who operated a small grocery store, he was again left as an orphan at sixteen when these foster parents died. The house and grocery store had been sold, and he would have been destitute except that folks of some friends allowed him to stay at their home.

At the age of twenty-two while making his living in various types of farm jobs, Bayardo became "born again" at the Missionary Pentecostal Church in his hometown and was baptized with water. Three months later in another locality, he received the baptism of the Holy Spirit. Then, for a few months, he remained in a larger city where he participated in fellowship with other believers for Missionary Bible Training before taking on the task of laboring in one of many communities where his church was organizing.

It was to this Momotombo area where Bayardo went in 1982 as a commissioned Lay Teacher. From one of the twenty-three members, he was given a piece of land to cultivate and call his own. He was dedicated to Christian gospel duties whereby he and faithful local leaders would guide small groups of laymen in visiting the neighbors.

One day when Bayardo was alone, a patrol of soldiers stopped by and quizzed him as to why he and his friends were not participating in political meetings. Angry that Bayardo had not joined the local Sandinista Defense Committee, popularly known as the "Eyes and Ears of the Revolution," the patrol leader also wondered why his religious group had not taken up arms to fight for the country.

This sparring with the new lawmen usually involved Bayardo's meeting different men within each army patrol. The single exception was the patrol leader who served as spokesman for every visit and commanded the base at La Paz Centro about fifteen miles from the entrance to the spacious Momotombo area. This officer knew who Bayardo was, calling him a "Protestant" and calling his friends Evangelical Christians.

During two subsequent encounters, the commandante continued haranguing the neighbor-to-neighbor visitation teams as drift-abouts and "street people going about fooling people with junk." The commandante was training his young troops to be good revolutionaries.

Soldiers scouted the Momotombo region, entering it in large trucks and then dividing into smaller units for patrol duty among the *campesino*[3] population. It was common knowledge that the troops were arresting anyone considered a dissenter to the Sandinista Party line.

For Bayardo and seven men of the local congregation who were holding a weekday planning session in the isolated chapel among the oak, pine, and cedar trees in the shadow of Mt. Momotombo, a showdown was about to take place. It would illustrate Sandinista policy in regard to any independent Christian thinking and convictions.

The men had arranged themselves in this small, rectangularly-designed worship sanctuary whose dimensions were something like seventeen by twenty-seven feet. The seating consisted of homemade, movable, wooden benches and chairs. The sanctuary walls were constructed with approximately three-by-three-foot openings, no window panes, with each space divided by a two-by-four holding the lower and upper wallboards.[4]

Suddenly, the familiar form of the pistol-packing commandante appeared with five young soldiers in tow, all carrying AK-47 rifles. Announcing that the place was surrounded with no possibility of escape, he declared,

"This evening will be your last. You are enemies of the revolution!" Then, hurling insults at the eight alarmed and unarmed men, labeling them "sons of bitches," "old dogs," and saying that their mothers were "whores," the Marxist-indoctrinated commandante shouted, "You deserve not to live. You are parasites of the revolution!"

With introductions over, the misguided one began to hit the hardy *campesinos* with his rifle butt and ordered his troops to follow suit.

The surprised men had no way of avoiding the blows. As in a nightmare, they heard the taunting jeers of the leader hounding them with "Where is your God? Call upon him! Can he save you?"

The church's leaders (elders, deacons, and Bayardo) received blows anywhere that a body could receive them: head, face, neck, chest, arms, stomach, ribs, groin, and back. They also were kicked.

Eventually, when all were subdued, lying prostrate, seriously wounded and bleeding on the floor with two already unconscious, the young soldiers began tying their prey and laughing.

With hands bound behind their backs and their feet secured so they could not move, the next important lesson of the revolution was administered. Gasoline was thrown at the side of the building, most of it splashing through the windows and sprinkling the subdued.

Knowing that death was near, some of the humiliated and burdened men wept while others encouraged one another with words such as, "It doesn't matter. We die in the service of the Lord. And if we have to be killed, it's better to have followed God's will!"

The very last words were spoken by Ramon Lopez, who exclaimed, "Don't be afraid! Our physical bodies may burn and we die, but our souls go to be with the Lord."

As the commandante ignited the fire, his death knell words were, "These dogs will die burnt!"

With flames inundating the chapel, Bayardo felt the passing of an unceasing interval of time. But, then, discovering that his bonds had burned in such a way that allowed him to free his hands and feet, quickly he moved

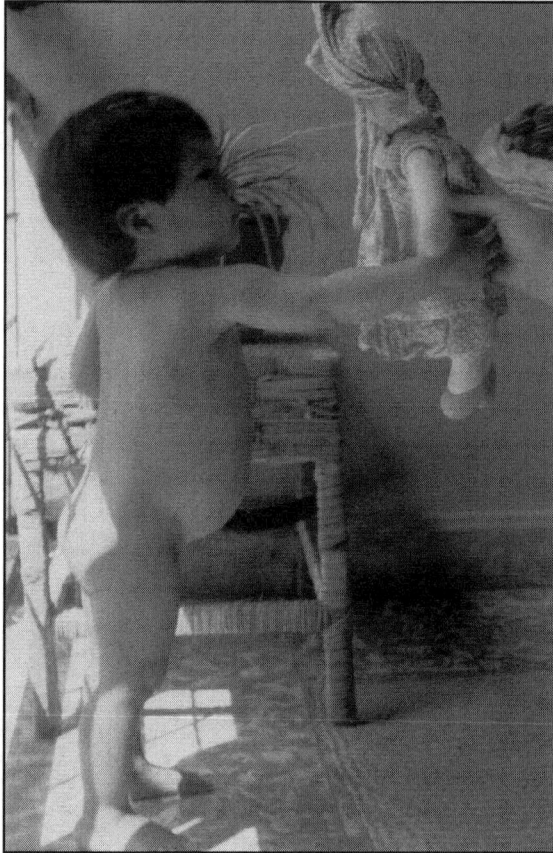

A child in need of treatment in Danli, El Paraiso, Honduras.

through the nearest open portion of a burning wall. In his dash for air and freedom, he caught a glimpse of one brother crawling out on his hands and knees. Though Bayardo kept running as if by sheer instinct, he glanced backward to see the crawling one finally stop and fall to the ground.

Noticing that the soldiers already had left, he could only concentrate upon distancing himself from the place with as much ground as possible. But over half a mile away, he too, headlong and helpless, fell upon the volcanic soil under the branches of a large cedar tree. He lay for five days where he had fallen.

The following personal information is what he remembered of the martyred: Francis Estrada, forty-five years old, left a wife and seven children; Ramon Lanusa, thirty-eight, left behind a wife and four children; Ramon Lopez, twenty-eight to thirty years, whose widow remained with three children; Misael Gutierrez, twenty; and Epifano and two other men who were single.

Bayardo lay with third-degree burns on his face, ears, hands, forearm,legs, and portions of his back. Due to the posture he had been forced to assume while tied during the atrocity, his stomach remained untouched, along with his feet and ankles where work shoes had served as a protection.

Because of continuous pain, Bayardo had no sense of passing time. There was no position in which he could find comfort. Rain which filtered through the cedar branches gave some relief. As rain flowed past his head, Bayardo even made an attempt to sip some. Mosquitoes bit him, but he didn't feel them. Though they made lots of noise, the intensity of his pain outdid any competition.

Shortly before noon on the fifth day, two *campesinos*, who happened to be fervent believers in Christ, came along the mountain trail and spotted him. Their first words were, "What happened?"

Though his face and tongue were severely swollen, Bayardo managed to mumble, "God was with me."

These farmers grasped him by his uninjured armpits and feet. Though his pain was excruciating, he was carried to the home of one of the men. A third committed brother in the Lord also became involved, and all tended to Bayardo's need for a month. This included applying medication and exemplary care.

What a burden Bayardo must have been to the families who assisted him! When one contemplates the many aspects associated with such pathos, the checking of the wounds, food, clothing, laundry, and toilet requirements, to say nothing of the security dangers, anyone's faith would have been tested.

Gausimos camp refugees, Jacaleapa, El Paraiso, Honduras.

As army units continued arresting individuals, Bayardo began to hear of friends who had been taken. In these cases, the authorities could produce no proof of guilt and, after two months, decided that these people would be released.

Bayardo was eventually attended to at a place of special care for a number of days before being secreted away to new and different locations for further recuperation.

In 1983, members of a Freedom Fighter unit found out about the great personal danger Bayardo was facing if he were discovered. He was asked if he would consider leaving Nicaragua. As his answer was in the affirmative, Bayardo was taken through three more communities before crossing the border at La Lodosa, Honduras, and from there directly to a Nicaraguan refugee camp.[5]

Introduction by President Reagan

When a friend was asked by the FDN to inquire if Bayardo would accept an invitation to tell his story in the States, he agreed and was flown to Washington, D.C.

What an experience he had! The highlight of this month's visit included a dinner in which he sat among six hundred Americans at a fund-raising drive for Nicaraguan refugees and was introduced to the group by none other than President Ronald Reagan.[1]

At the meeting's conclusion, Bayardo met the Rev. Pat Robertson, President of the Christian Broadcasting Network (CBN) and host of its televised *700 Club* program, who made a promise to help Bayardo in the matter of plastic surgery.

Though the impression of the American news media was not complimentary, this did not detract from Bayardo's appreciation. "I never thought the Lord would have taken me to such a beautiful country."

After an interval of about eight months, Bayardo was broughtto Norfolk, Virginia, where Dr. Charles E. Horton did corrective surgery in the area of Bayardo's mouth and chin, improvement of the restructuring of his right ear, and amputated a portion of the little finger of his left hand.

Bayardo said, "I will always remember Pat Robertson as a man with a good heart."

Bayardo continues to live in a refugee camp about ninety kilometers east of the capital of Honduras where he has his own space in a windowless wooden hut with a dirt floor. The food supply under the United Nations refugee organization is really not adequate and the water supply is polluted.[2]

Bayardo has great concern for those left behind in Nicaragua. Yet he has no valid passport, like many thousands of Nicaraguan citizens, and is therefore stateless and cannot immigrate anywhere.

Aleksandr Solzhenitsyn, the great Russian writer, once made a statement quoted in the *Congressional Record* on January 28, 1982: "All of Marxism is based on hatred of religion."[3]

Frank and Tere Bendana

Tegucigalpa, Francisco Morazan, Honduras

December 7, 1986

> Frank and Tere left Nicaragua as displaced persons. Their
> property and place in society were stolen in a way which
> would not have been acceptable if such injustice had hap-
> pened within the United States.

Grabbing for Power

FRANK: I was born in New York City in 1935. My father, a Nicaraguan by
birth, already had been made a naturalized American citizen. My mother,
a first generation Lithuanian born in America, came from Pennsylvania.

Moving with my family to Nicaragua in 1947 at the age of twelve, I
became totally bilingual in Spanish and English. After graduation from the
Pan American Agricultural School in the Zamorano Valley of Honduras, I
returned to Nicaragua where Tere and I married. Receiving a scholarship
to study at the University of Florida, I left with Tere for the States the same
year as our marriage. This coincided with my parent's return to the States
and my father's service as the Nicaraguan Vice-Consul in New York.

TERE: My name is Maria Teresa McEwan de Bendana, and I was born in
Nicaragua. Although the McEwan name comes from a Scottish grandfather, my mother and father were both born in Nicaragua.

My father was trained for a military career by the United States Marines.
Later, not appreciating a trend which the Nicaraguan National Guard took
under the Somoza regime and wanting to be more independent, he left the
Guard in 1947 with the rank of captain. Entering the field of coffee farming in
his hometown area of Matagalpa, he worked very diligently, invested wisely
and, eventually prospering, remained there until his death.

Our married life began with Frank's eight years of study in the States.
This included six in Florida where he earned his Ph.D. in Biochemistry and
Plant Physiology and two in Connecticut where he did post-doctoral work

Frank and Tere Bendana.

at Yale. In 1965 our family went to Leon, Nicaragua, where for one year Frank taught biochemistry and biology at the Autonomous National University of Nicaragua. Due to both economic and political factors, raising a large family and not liking the University's left-leaning political tendencies, Frank became employed, first with Standard Oil of New Jersey and then as a partner with four other owners in an agricultural-chemical corporation in Corinto, Nicaragua.

FRANK: In 1968, Tere's father gave us 280 *manzanas,* a 490-acre piece of land, near Matagalpa takeover. It was producing 5,000 *quintals* of coffee, one *quintal* equaling one hundred pounds, and was considered a model farm.

TERE: After Frank earned his degrees, I said, "It is my turn to go to school." So, in Managua I received degrees in education and psychology from the University of Central America (UCA) and was hired as a school counselor.

A Catholic girls school I had once attended served as a contact for my keeping in touch with parents of former students who wished to keep this facility operating. Some of our children had been enrolled there, but the school was closed, mainly because of the earthquake damage in 1972. Despite this, parents continued using the school's parents' organizational name, Parent Teachers Organization (PTO), and began negotiating a transfer of the school's control from the Sisters of the Assumption Congregation. They hired me to become the principal, or director as the title is used in Nicaragua. Beginning in 1975, I worked in this position for seven years.

VERN: Is this school still functioning?

TERE: Yes, it still belongs to the parents who want a traditional education for their children. As far as I am aware, the government hasn't taken it over.[1] What has been holding authorities back, basically, is that they can't afford the expense of such an educational operation. However, they do control what is being taught.

Because the government allowed religious education, Frank and I chose to remain in Nicaragua. As agriculture and education were basic for the nation, we knew that our presence was needed.

Frank had been working with a friend of ours, a Nicaraguan named Jorge Salazar. Both of them had been very active in organizing coffee cooperatives, 7,000 members in the Matagalpa area alone, which included large growers, though the majority were medium-sized and smaller. However, whereas Frank was rudely expelled from the country, Jorge already had been killed by the Sandinistas.

FRANK: One of the first acts of the new government was the confiscation of the fertilizer company with the excuse that the four other owners had been close to Somoza. We in the private sector had not counted on this turn of events when we concentrated our efforts to overthrow Somoza.

Anyway, I now had extra time to try to undo what I had assisted to create in our country, the takeover by a partisan group with some very strange ideas. My activities were centered, mainly, in the formation of non-partisan farm organizations—co-ops, associations, and trade unions—until June 30, 1981.

That morning I left my home in Managua at eight o'clock. While on the way to work, I was stopped by government police, put under arrest, asked to make some ridiculous statements, which I did not do, and was forcibly placed on an airliner bound for Mexico. Deported and thrown out, not even sent back to the United States, my country of origin, I had been deprived of all rights.

The best definition I've heard of Communism was given to me by our family friend and ex-Communist, Humberto Belli, when he said, "Communism is the idolatry of power."

VERN: Had he chosen to go along with Communist ideology, Humberto could have had much power in Nicaragua.

FRANK: Definitely, Humberto gives testimony of the Lord, who did not reveal Himself personally but showed a need for him to change.[2] As he had become estranged from his wife and children, which is no small thing, either, he realized that he should change and, instead of spreading propaganda for the left, commenced to carry out the word of the Lord.

VERN: In one of his books, he quotes verse[3] written by his sister. Is she still a Communist today?

FRANK: Gioconda Belli is an extreme Leftist. She is one of the pure ideologues of Nicaragua who accused her brother of being an instrument of Capitalism and Imperialism.

Before he decided to leave the country, Humberto strongly criticized and denounced the regime.

VERN: Is it correct to say that when the Left gets into power, it uses men as cannon fodder?

FRANK: They'll use them as firewood or anything else that serves their purpose of all-inclusive control. These power-hungry humans make up reasons for everything they do. They're adroit liars, know no morality, and feel they can go about saying and doing what they wish.[4]

VERN: What were some of your impressions when you saw the new officials come into office?

FRANK: Because of their skill in disguising their pretensions and feelings, these individuals seemed to be good for the country. Among them were those that all of us knew to be good professionals. What we did not know was that many of them had great weaknesses which were being exploited. If one were a drug addict, that person would be given drugs and made into a greater addict so the givers of the "goodies" could do what they wanted. If not, that which was dear would be taken away. If one were a homosexual, they would cater to the taste. If one were power-hungry, they would give power. For any of the human needs which one can think of, including religion, Communists will accommodate as long as benefits can be gained.

The Catholic Popular Church[5] in Nicaragua functions as a good example of this adaptation. Given enough time, it will try to create a schism, now that it has gained a few members[6] and will foster this new found strength having as its only requirement that converts be faithful to its doctrine, but completely.

Communists and American Politics

VERN: Did you know Tomas Borge?

FRANK: Not personally. I knew of him and individuals who grew up with him. One of the original members of the Sandinista National Liberation Front, the last one alive, and the one given the post of Interior Minister, he is a person very much to be reckoned with.

The following story reveals something about him and the Communist mind. While being trailed by the National Guard, Borge tried to perpetrate a robbery. Having been foiled in the attempt and fleeing, he ran into a Managua shopping center where he came upon a short man like himself who was dressed in a National Guard uniform. Without asking any question or saying anything, Borge turned toward the man, shot and killed him.

Having exhausted his bullets, he yelled to everyone in the center, "I'm Tomas Borge! They're going to take me prisoner!" With these words, he attempted to create a reaction among the public so that Somoza could not cause his disappearance.

While Tomas was in custody, Jose Esteban Gonzalez, the President of the Permanent Commission on Human Rights of Nicaragua(CPDH) visited him a number of times. Jose Esteban assured Tomas and Nicaraguans in general that Tomas would not be tortured nor mistreated in any way.

Some years later when Jose Esteban did not follow all the policies of the new leaders and kept to his own way of thinking, as a just and moral man is wont to do, the Sandinistas threw him into confinement. When Tomas came by to see him, he was reminded by Jose Esteban,[1] "Tomas, I feel that I should have, at least, the same minimal treatment that you received."

Tomas answered Jose Esteban with strong words, *"Hijo de puta,"* which in translation from Spanish would mean something like "son of a whore," or "son of a bastard," but even stronger than that, and concluded with words that meant "The times are different."

The West makes a gross mistake when it believes that Communist leaders will react appropriately if given "the right time and circumstances." It simply is not true. I, personally, know of no example in our recent world history where one can find any sort of benevolent and just action from such leaders as long as they weren't forced to do so.[2]

VERN: You witnessed in 1979-1981 at close range a Communist takeover of a country in our Western Hemisphere.

FRANK: Though many in the United States still refuse to believe this, Humberto Ortega [Saavedra], the Minister of Defense, stated in August 1980 that the people of Nicaragua had elected the form of government they wanted. While not falling back into bourgeois[3] elections that other countries used, Nicaragua would have them in five years.[4] No new party, however, would have the possibility of taking leadership. Elections would only be for the same party functionaries vying for different positions.

Daniel Ortega [Saavedra][5], the assassin, kidnapper, and bank robber[6], was not elected President by the Nicaraguan people. He was placed in that position by his party in that mock 1984 election.

VERN: With few American leaders willing to accept the Nicaraguan Communist takeover, why is there not more seriousness in the general American political stance?

FRANK: This is politics, but who takes the brunt of it? In Nicaragua I met Jim Wright, Bill Alexander, Chris Dodd,[7] and I don't remember how many more Democrats and Republicans who realized what was going on. Unfortunately, this knowledge that could have been used for the good of the American people did not further the personal political future of these men.

On February 25, 1982, I and three others testified before the Senate Subcommittee on Western Hemisphere Affairs of the United States Senate. Two were pro-Left and two of us were not.[8]

Among the pro-Left was Miss Andrea I. Young, the daughter of Atlanta's mayor who had just completed his time as the United States Ambassador to the United Nations. She spoke with authority because she had just spent six days in Nicaragua. As a guest of the Sandinista government who made sure that she saw and heard whatever it wanted from her, she returned to the States with an air of proprietorship.

Known for his Leftist inclinations there also appeared William M. Leo Grande, Director of Political Science in the School of Government and Public Administration at the American University in Washington, D.C.

The third person was Bruce McColm, Director of the Caribbean Basin Project at Freedom House in New York.

Each of us was to make a short statement. Senators were to ask questions. When my turn came, most of our Democratic friends got up and left. Those called out[9] included Senator Christopher Dodd. The only one who remained was the committee Sub-Chairman, Republican Senator Jesse Helms from North Carolina.

I began by implying that our senators would not be present because I was not going to speak about human rights but about human wrongs. Senator Dodd, who had spoken and appeared so knowledgeable on Nicaragua, would not be there to argue these points against me. I knew that he knew that I was right.

Vern, it is horrible to say so, but these leaders were saying that it makes "good politics" to take away the focus of the atrocities and terrible wrongs that are happening to neighbors next door who depend upon the United States. If we have learned anything in the twentieth century, we can ask, "What is the power behind politics?" The answer returns the same as Machiavelli, Richelieu, and Cain knew.[10]

With all of the partisan tendencies of the press, one finds very little Freedom Fighter abuse. The western press, of course, won't emphasize that there is a civil war going on in Nicaragua and that its people are struggling to regain freedoms which they had under the government of Somoza.[11]

In 1979 when the new government came into power, it killed and imprisoned National Guard personnel.[12] Illegally, the new leaders subjected these men to torture and brainwashing for doing a job which any working person would have done under similar circumstances.

At the end of the Somoza government, of the approximately 6,000 members of the Guard remaining, both active and reserve, some 1,200 to 1,500 were killed in the fighting, more than 2,000 fled to the United States, about

500 remained in Central America, and roughly 150-200 joined the Freedom Fighters with barely a handful of officers among them.[13] This does not take into consideration the last-minute volunteers who aided the Guard in the final days before Somoza's fall. Nevertheless, since it has been over seven years since the robbing of the Revolution in Nicaragua, how many Guardsmen would still be fighting within the ranks of the Freedom Fighters?

The Freedom Fighters have always been made up of working people, farmers and farm workers who do not want to live under Communism and lose the possibility for freedoms that those within the United States enjoy.[14] Some leaders within the States seem to believe in a war according to comic book standards where the good guys can defend themselves with wooden swords against real bullets. It is shocking but true.[15] In the reality of warfare, the goal should be to terminate and win as soon as possible.[16] If not, all will perish.

The Name, Contra

VERN: Former President Reagan preferred to use the term "Freedom Fighter," but the media has gone against him on this. It instead prefers to use the term which Communists like: "Contra."

FRANK: People of the Left are very astute in maintaining and re-using terminology and methods which have been useful for them.[1] Wouldn't one agree that it is much more preferable to say, "I'm pro-democratic" than to say, "I'm anti-communistic"? The media presents us as anti-Communist and thus places us in a negative position.

At the death of Jorge Salazar,[2] I became the spokesman for the strongest organized group in Nicaragua, the coffee growers. I had been an active worker with the Matagalpa Coffee Growers Association and then became President of the National Union of Nicaraguan Coffee Growers (UNCAFENIC).

Even before Jorge's death, he and I worked with something the Left feared. We had numbers. On many occasions we were able to hold a rally or meeting where we'd fill up a theater with three thousand participants.

Considering the restrictions on travel to and from our gatherings, this was quite a feat.

The government attempted to divide the large coffee growers' group in Matagalpa by not allowing the growers to utilize the word "cooperative" in its name. This constituted a lame excuse to deny our very democratic organization the rightful description of what we were, a cross-section of independent coffee growers with a gamut of farm acreage and productive capabilities. Asserting that the word "cooperative" could only pertain to a homogenous mass of small farmers, it forced us to change our name, "Central Co-op of Coffee Growers of Matagalpa," to "Matagalpa Coffee Growers' Association" (Asociacion de Cafetaleros de Matagalpa).

TERE: The government tried hard to dissuade the smaller growers and kept telling them that they had no business in such meetings. So, it was moving to hear how the campesinos, even the old men among them, would stand up waving their sombreros and enthusiastically express their feelings. I heard of one who had spoken out saying, "Why does the government want to disunite us? We are all together as coffee growers. In the past these larger growers helped us when banks wouldn't lend us the money to raise our crops."

VERN: When was this meeting held?

TERE: There were meetings such as this in Matagalpa toward the end of 1979 and into the beginning of 1980.

FRANK: Jaime Wheelock, the Sandinista Minister of Agriculture and Agrarian Reform, was forced to witness how the rich and poorer growers respected each other and worked together for the welfare of the country, not just for a single party. Observing how Jorge had the support of all the members, Jaime's party took its vengeance a year later on November 17, 1980, when it assassinated Jorge with enough bullets to make sure that he would die. One bullet even entered the bottom of one foot and went up the leg; this in a country with no capital punishment. He left a wife and three children, the youngest, a boy of sixteen.

At the time of his death, Jorge was Acting President of the Superior Council for Private Enterprise (COSEP)[3] and the President of the Union of

Agricultural Growers and Cattlemen's Associations of Nicaragua (UPANIC). UPANIC included, among other groups, the coffee, rice, cotton, and sorghum growers and cattle ranchers. It belonged to COSEP, the umbrella for the whole private business sector which covered not only private agricultural organizations but also businesses not connected to the government. Tens of thousands of people were represented.

After the death of Jorge, the state began setting another deadly trap for the coffee growers and myself.

"Keep Quiet"

TERE: Everyone kept telling my husband "You'll have to be careful! Don't talk too much," but he was not to be intimidated and continued publishing his opinions on behalf of the coffee growers.

The week before Frank was thrown out, a friend said, "They are about to confiscate that which is yours. You'd better shut up. Keep quiet for the sake of your wife and kids."

I didn't want him to do this for my sake. I admired his courage and didn't want him to muzzle himself, though the government was continually accusing him of reactionary wrongs against the state and searching for ways to expel him.

FRANK: The government began coaching their lackeys to make denunciations against the coffee growers in publications and newspapers. These articles alleged that harassment was being promoted by our association, which had an American tourist as its president. Four days before my expulsion, it was reported that murders had been committed in a certain part of the country. The alleged murderers had been interrogated, and it was discovered that the deeds had been instigated and paid for by the Matagalpa Coffee Growers' Association.

I was being set up. It would have been very easy for anyone to shoot me as I drove up to the farm. The government would have had no trouble reporting that an irate relative of one of those "poor murdered victims" simply took justice into his own hands.

As an answer to these events, I was in the process of going to court to sue the newspaper, *Barricada*, and the Sandinista Television System for libel and injury of my person.

It was plain to see what the Sandinistas were up to, but the strategy that UPANIC, our lawyers, and myself were taking still had to be discussed thoroughly. We were dealing with people who play for keeps.

The day I was detained, an official handed me a statement in which the authorities wanted me to publicly renounce my American citizenship, denounce all private business sector organizations as directed by and funded through the CIA[1] under the guidance of the American Embassy, and express remorse in having deceived the Nicaraguan people. If I did this, the Director of Immigration said that I would be given the opportunity to apply for Nicaraguan citizenship.

After I refused to sign, the Director Mario Mejia pulled out another prepared sheet which had come from the office of Tomas Borge. It was my expulsion order.

Had I decided to negotiate and sign the first document, the party would have published my resignation and denouncement and kicked me out of the country anyway.

VERN: You were accused of meddling and goaded because you were in the country on an American passport.

FRANK: By Nicaraguan law, I was a Nicaraguan. Being born the son of a Nicaraguan citizen and residing in the country more than five continuous years between the ages of twelve to twenty-one made me a citizen by adoption. I didn't have to do anything to prove this. In 1950, I played with the Nicaraguan basketball team at the Guatemalan Olympics. No one would have thought that I was not a Nicaraguan.

I did have a Permanent Residence Visa, as I had chosen to use an American passport which Nicaraguan law permitted.

The country's present officials carry out different actions in order to fulfill its desire for power. These leaders do it as recognized government policy, and promote it without the moral reasoning that Judeo-Christian values would include.[2]

Tensions are tools that enhance Communist power. Tension serves as an excuse for Communist governments to have large armies to repress and intimidate citizens within their own respective countries. Cuba uses it for furthering Communist power in Central and South America, even in Africa.

In Managua there exists water rationing three times a week, and a person doesn't get food at reasonable prices unless he holds a ration card, which has to be obtained from the local Block Committee (CDS) chairperson. This rationing is not truly needed. It's done because of the power utilized in telling people when to eat, when not to eat, and what to eat. Long food distribution lines cause a good Communist to smile because it shows his system is operating properly.[3]

The Communist system, however, deals with more than rationing. Citizens have to give up their children and all freedoms and must do as they are told. The individual becomes a "lump" or a "something" and loses individuality. They are not telling you, Vern, nor me, Frank. They are saying, "You people, go!"[4]

In creating conditions to increase his power, the Communist also acquires a rationale which liberates him from guilt. When he is committing a crime, he does not perpetrate it as an individual but as part of a mass operation, a necessary clean-up job. There is nothing about which he should feel guilty.[5]

This is the way life is handled by the leaders in Nicaragua. Someone arguing in their favor might ask, "Why would they allow a guy like Frank into their country? He's a pain in their necks!"

On the same wavelength, why should I allow an assassin like Nora Astorga into the United States as Nicaraguan Ambassador to the United Nations? She is a prostitute who seduced General Perez[6] to leave his bodyguards, go into her chambers, and in her bed, nude, be assassinated.

After the fall of Somoza, she talked openly about what she had done. The *La Prensa* newspaper in Managua brought out the facts.

New Indoctrination

VERN: Would you reveal reflections as to the role played by Catholic clergy in Nicaragua?

I once attented a meeting at the University of Minnesota Newman Center where I witnessed individuals selling *Barricada* newspapers and signing up citizens to support Leftist rebels in El Salvador. This sort of emphasis, I'm afraid, is taking place in a number of Christian denominations.[1]

FRANK: Revealing a confused American interpretation of democracy, this happens to be the same thinking that controlled the meeting at the Medellin conference[2] where a minor but strong American liberal faction prevailed. What one finds in the States are confused men and women who'll run something like the Newman group and think they are really accomplishing good in their social activism. For them the Nicaraguan Revolution has taken that country out of the clothes of the demon, Somoza, and they are now encouraging others to aid its new leaders.

Let us look at what Communists promote in an attempt to understand this new breed[3] of religious confusion. Communists always begin an argument by saying that they are not being given all of their freedoms, especially, the right to dissent. Yet, when they seize power, the first liberty they themselves take away is the liberty to dissent. One does not know of a Communist regime where one can say that Communism is wrong.

VERN: As I hadn't laughed, smiled nor clapped when the group did, when leaving that campus meeting, I intentionally was not given a program of coming events.

FRANK: We are looking at a religious constituency who are malcontent and are forcefully saying that the wrongs which they see are someone else's fault, not theirs.

Father Fernando Cardenal,[4] now Secretary of Education and Secretary General of the Sandinista Youth, preached, "You cannot be a Catholic if you are not a Sandinista." He said this at a Managua church in May 1980 during a Memorial Mass for a friend who had been killed by the National Guard.

VERN: Did you notice the procession of moves to the Popular Church?

FRANK: It was my impression that it was done, mainly, through the Jesuit[5]-administered Catholic university which hired many of its professors from among clergy outside of Nicaragua who had been influenced by the Left. In the late sixties and early seventies, the Socialist teachings from these professors went into the high school levels.

There was a priest, Uriel Molina,[6] from a family in Matagalpa with whom Tere was acquainted, who used to have a study group living with him. What we didn't know about him was that he was indoctrinating Catholic youth with Marxism and starting Communist cells, so that today he is counted as one of the vanguard of the Popular Church.

Nicaragua was not being singled out for this new stress. The practice of such church-oriented people continues in the States as well. Let me suggest to all that are reading this interview to be sure to check what their children are learning and to remind other parents to do the same. No denomination is immune from the danger that turned to a tragedy in Nicaragua.

There were changes in the liturgy. We heard Spanish instead of Latin, which was great! We were singing different hymns and melodies. All dovetailed very nicely with the so-called "preferential option for the poor."[7] All the circumstances congealed and the Left had everything they needed, a ready religion with religious people in place.[8]

The following words were part of the whole scam: "This political machine couldn't be so bad. With it came so-and-so who is a priest." There appeared upon the scene such clergy as Miguel D'Escoto Brockman, a Maryknoll; the Cardenals, Ernesto (a regular priest) and his brother, Fernando. a Jesuit; Uriel Molina; and others.[9]

There were ninety-nine others who were behaving as they should and toiling in genuine missionary work, but all at once one was inundated with a plethora of orders, congregations, priests and sisters with designs on some sort of power.

Of late, I'm very pleased to observe that the Catholic Church in Nicaragua is maintaining its position as over against the Popular Church.[10]

VERN: Tere, would you add to Frank's insights?

TERE: Devotion for the Blessed Virgin Mary is very strong. The day Catholics celebrate the Immaculate Conception worldwide, December 8, is a national holiday in Nicaragua.

In tune with this feeling, the government began to present Mary as an activist. It featured her as one who worked in her neighborhood and helped those who needed aid, such as a social worker would do. Posters were displayed depicting Mary with braided hair and fitted with a smart, cute-looking, little campesino hat and wearing a Latin American woman's dress, a picture never seen before.

A nun pointedly noted how Mary would fit very nicely into any CDS group.

Frank Gone/School Duties

VERN: With Frank gone a new turn of events for you.

TERE: That's an understatement.

When Frank was forced to make his exit in '81, the Land Reform Law stated that if Nicaraguan citizens left the country for more than six months, they automatically lost all of their property and rights of citizenship.

A private person could own a coffee farm up to 500 *manzanas* [875 acres] and up to 1,000 *manzanas* [1,750 acres] for cattle raising. In April 1982, over ten months after my husband's exile, I noticed in *Barricada* the newly listed farm confiscations which had been chosen as a result of decisions from Jaime Wheelock. Our farm was on this list, the first time our family knew of such action.

Our farm comprised 280 *manzanas*, much below the Agrarian Reform law limit. As this allowed for the right of appeal before the courts, I searched and found a lawyer and commenced a lawsuit, but our case was not brought to trial.

Then, we heard that the authorities had sent a special proposal requesting that the State Council[1] (Consejo de Estado) declare our farm a "Public Utility" (*Por Razones de Utilidad Publica*). But their plan didn't pass the Council!

Anyway, it's been seized. We don't know the legal reason. They do what they want.

VERN: Would you introduce me to your school duties?

TERE: There was a name change from Assumption School (*Colegio de las Asuncion*) to Annunciation School (*Colegio de la Anunciacion*).

The many duties at the girls' school included responsibilities with the parents and scheduling changes in the educational program.

VERN: Were any of the former nuns working at the school?

TERE: We did secure the services of one sister who wanted to work with us. She was placed in charge of the school's religious instruction.

We had no official school priest, but Mass was offered once a week.

VERN: What was the school's enrollment?

TERE: Four hundred girls before Somoza left. Afterwards, as parents began leaving, it dropped to less than 350.

VERN: Which grades did it include?

TERE: A complete system from kindergarten through high school.

VERN: You had relationships with other secondary schools?

TERE: Representing the parents in Managua, I kept in contact with other Catholic schools and was active in the Catholic Association of Private Schools. This included the Jesuits' school and the Christian Brothers with their Educational Institute of Managua. These were the two largest private schools for boys in Nicaragua. There also were two congregations of nuns who conducted private schools for girls, the Teresian Academy (Colegio Teresiano) and the Pureza de Maria.

Touted Literacy Program

VERN: With reference to the publicity bash that the Left gave the world in 1980 in the form of the Nicaraguan Literacy Campaign, were the religious schools affected?

TERE: Within all of our religious schools, there were members of the Sandinista Youth organization[1] who did whatever the government wanted from them. The majority, however, together with their religious and lay teach-

ers, felt obligated to do something for those who did not know how to read
and willingly went to the rural areas. Some took along their Bibles and used
the time for evangelization purposes.

VERN: I've heard that the Literacy Campaign served as a method for intro-
ducing Marxism to the masses.

TERE: This Literacy Campaign was financed from within the United States
but controlled by the Cubans.[2]

Composed of twenty-two lessons, the text was printed in Cuba and
embraced the teaching method of the Brazilian educator Paulo Freire.[3]

In spite of the fact that up to ninety percent of the Nicaraguan population is Catholic, there was no mention of God, church, or anything about
religion.

"Well," the government would retort, "this is not a religious book. We
are teaching reading and writing, not religion."

VERN: No religion is a religion.

TERE: With only three or four months to study, the great majority did not
learn beyond a first grader's ability. With the government striving to
demonstrate to the world how effective it could be in solving a social problem, it gave orders to instructors that everyone in each class had to pass the
literacy test. There never was a follow-up study, and there never would be.[4]

VERN: What did the young student teachers from your school think about
the Agrarian Reform?

TERE: For many it didn't bother them. They thought the government was
going to give land to the poor. There was no realization that a Communist
process was unfolding itself.[5]

Leadership has been offering schools, hospitals, and all of paradise but
are not delivering. Who are the worse off? The campesinos!

Officials have opened a store in Managua where one can purchase every-
thing from eggs, milk, and bread to refrigerators and TV sets. It is called
"The Diplomatic Store" and reserved for the privileged few who buy with
U.S. dollars.[6] But what happened concerning promises to the poor?

VERN: The Literacy Campaign must have been one gigantic interruption for the educational program of your school.

TERE: All school operations were shut down.

The 1979 school year which normally would have run from February to November had to be extended to February of 1980 due to the war during the previous summer months. But it was rescheduled to commence in June due to the Literacy Campaign in the spring.

I asked the state education officials, "What are you going to do with the rest of the children who don't go out on the Literacy Campaign? What about the wasted time, especially, for the elementary grades?"

They didn't care.

"Terrible Were Those Days for the Private Schools"

TERE: The Literacy Campaign dates were again revised so it would be concluded in August, and it was announced that the 1980 school year was to begin in August or September. But further confusion followed when government education personnel discovered that schools in Central American countries began in February. This caused the 1980 school year to finally end in November of 1981.

VERN: How many girls within your care belonged to the Sandinista Youth organization?

TERE: Forty-five.

VERN: How did they conduct themselves?

TERE: They were under direct orders and supervision of party bosses who sent information to them as to how they were to conduct themselves. These girls were an organized military unit who made it their business to discover what was going on in school affairs and dispatch these details to government officials.

When the girls of this organization began interrupting classes, I complained to the Ministry of Education. Though I should have gone to the Sandinista Party, how far could I have gotten?

The ministry agreed that the girls had to respect the classroom, but thought they should be permitted to do their political activity during recess.

Visitors from the Sandinista Youth office entered the school grounds and party propaganda was placed upon the bulletin board and classroom walls: photos, newspaper clippings, and assorted bits and pieces.

Have you ever seen a university that has been taken over by the Left? Its walls look dirty and are full of graffiti. The city of Managua is a showcase for graffiti, bulletins, slogans on walls, etc., including the public buildings.

Terrible were these days for the private schools, including one incident in which the authorities actually placed a student from another school in jail. Because the democratic party caucuses and the committed Christian girls of our school wanted to protest this action, their leaders declared, "We are planning a strike this morning and will not be attending classes."

"Okay," I relented, "but do this in a quiet manner. You just want your voice to be heard in that you are worried about the plight of this detained student."

Though I promptly closed the gates of the school, one of the Sandinista Youth sneaked off the school grounds and informed its office concerning the demonstration in process.

The Party dispatched the Divine Mobs[1], so named *Turbas Divinas* by Daniel Ortega. Our schoolgirls began to cry out, "The Turbas are coming! The Turbas are coming!"

The Mob came yelling and screaming to the school with the usual accompaniment of photographers and TV cameramen with them. Because policemen were there, I walked to the gates and pleaded with one of them, "Send this mob away! This is a private school and it's not disturbing any-one else. It's your job to put order into the place!"

He simply said, "We do not protect the bourgeois." This policeman was telling me that our school did not represent the working class and would not aid me.

Meanwhile, the Mob pushed against the gate with so much pressure that it was forced open and in poured the uninvited. My students began fighting the Mob.

VERN: What was the composition of this mob?

TERE: Among them were high school students, especially those in institutions conducted by the state sector, the public schools and college students. Along with these were older adults, men and women, with the women predominant.

This was the first of two incidents (it happened to be the only situation when I was present) when the Mob was sent to our school. With thankfulness to God, no one sustained any bodily injury nor was there any property damage to speak of.

The next ruckus occurred while I was away in Costa Rica where I had placed two of my boys in a school. This time both bodily injury and property damage took place, as the Mob broke windows and roughed up the President of our Student Body. Upon my return, I saw her bruises.

VERN: How old was she?

TERE: Eighteen, and in her last year of high school, a very brave girl. The Physical Education instructor and one of the Math teachers, both male, came to her rescue. Approximately fifteen Mob members had been beating her.

Liberation Theology

VERN: Let's turn our attention to the church's religious leadership.

TERE: In the past Jesuit communities administered boys' schools whose students were chosen from high society's cream of the crop. Thirty years ago the most able of these was given the title, "Perpetual Prince."

I have heard and agree that the Jesuits developed a guilty conscience and opted for the poor.

The Jesuit and Maryknoll Fathers were the main resource groups for bringing Liberation Theology into Nicaragua. I attended one of the Jesuit seminars for educators within the Catholic Church in which Fr. Gustavo

Gutierrez, the Peruvian author of *Liberation Theology*, was featured. As a principal, teacher, and parent, I took special opportunity to attend two of Fr. Gutierrez's lectures. At the time, I had two boys in the Jesuit school.

Claiming that a Christian could be a Marxist, Fr. Gutierrez reasoned that Marxism was merely a scientific method, a tool, for analyzing history.

During the question and answer session, I asked, "But Marxists don't believe in God. They are atheists. Is it not then incompatible for a Christian to be a Marxist?"

He entered into a lengthy explanation of how European theologians continue to meet once a year with Marxists for dialogue, stated that we humans did not have the right to own land, just as we could not own the air we breath nor the water we drink, and that natural resources were created by God for man to use but not to own.

When he finished, I still was unable to comprehend what he was talking about and could not accept his conclusion that a Christian could honestly be a Marxist.[1]

At the other lecture, a Jesuit scolded principals of private schools and made us feel guilty because we mostly worked with the high socio-economic group.

When the opportunity came for me to express myself, I said, "We are all children of God. Who is going to take care of the education of wealthy girls, if attention is shown only to the poor?"

The present rulers of Nicaragua called us, and I want to emphasize this ridiculous term, the "bourgeois" and compared us to the very rich of the world. But we, the "rich," were paying on a mortgage for our house, had a farm plus a bank loan. Our country didn't have "high-class society," not the likes of the Kennedys, Rockefellers, and Vanderbilts. No one had that much money.

My father's father was an immigrant who worked in the mines. My father began working with coffee and eventually became a successful grower after forty years. Though he died one month after Frank was expelled, I'm glad his end came when it did. He would have suffered more and more as officials, little by little, were confiscating the product of years of toil, his land.

One of the farms taken away, with the reasoning that it was too large for one family, comprised cattle and coffee on 2,000 manzanas [3,500 acres]. The state attempted to confiscate another farm in an area where other properties were being taken, but, so far, this farm of my father's was the only one not appropriated.[2]

The school had many families from different strata of society, not just the wealthy. Religious schools did not appreciate the attempt on the part of state officeholders to instill hatred between the poor and the so-called rich.

Even though the Sandinistas claim that they don't want classes in society, they form their own and favor fights between these. For me, a hint of this occurred during the Somoza time when high school students demonstrated. I was one in a committee that went to see President Somoza to state the grievances. He was very cordial to our committee, and, after finding out what the problem entailed, asked an aide to do something about it. Later, after the problem was resolved, our committee was accused of being on the side of Somoza. It was then that I realized that the Left was behind the demonstration in the first place and were not interested in solving anything, only in causing unrest.

Because of my experience in Nicaragua, I have to state that there are priests who should not be priests but are Communist agents[3] sent to divide the church.

Within the Catholic Church in the States, I have noticed priests who are infiltrating it with similar liberal teachings which we were subjected to in Central America.[4]

Concerns Including the Pope's Visit

VERN: When you resigned to be with your husband, how did things finally conclude at the Annunciation School?

TERE: I found a lady to fill my position. My career as school Director came to an end in December of 1982 and I went to Costa Rica. Returning to

Nicaragua in January and then back to Costa Rica, I began making plans for the move to Texas.

VERN: The Pope visited Central America about that time, didn't he?

TERE: Yes, I delayed my departure some so I could witness this. In Costa Rica I watched the Nicaraguan television coverage but could hardly believe the manner in which he was being treated. The Mob shouted at him and demanded that he offer prayers for the fallen Sandinista soldiers[1] who died repelling the "imperialistic invaders," a reference to the civil war in progress.

VERN: Would you relate more of this story?

TERE: In May, I visited a nun in Nicaragua who had been at the open-air Mass in a position to observe the Mob in action. She belonged to a religious order that had been placed near to where the Pope was ministering.

Although the government had publicized the fact that it would provide transportation for all who wanted to attend, this sister said that the authorities required all to register in advance and used the transportation system to insure its control. Boarding a bus at a designated seminary, she was forced to take along a Sandinista Party flag as thousands of others were compelled to do.

During the Mass the sister was sandwiched close to a sub-commandante who was in charge of State Security and the Mob. He would signal the Mob as to when they should begin to shout and chant in a disruptive manner. She could hardly believe what she was seeing. The demonstration against the Pope came from a very small group that had loudspeakers and was aided by government television, radio, and audience mikes.

VERN: All cues were tightly controlled.

TERE: Definitely.

Other friends were situated far back in the massive audience. They had not been allowed to take along their white and yellow church flags, so they took out their handkerchiefs and waved them while singing their songs of praise to the Lord.

When those in the vast assembly saw and heard what their country's leaders had done, they were surprised and sickened.[2]

VERN: Why did you return to Nicaragua in May?

TERE: We heard friends and family in Nicaragua tell us, "You've been confiscated!"

Though the farm had been taken, we still had our house in Managua along with rental property. Before leaving the country I had rented our home to the Costa Rican Ambassador thinking that it would be safe in his hands. This house and the other one were both taken.

To prove that I had been away from the country within the legal period required by Sandinista law, I returned to Managua with my passport. But to no avail. The confiscation listed on May 13 in *La Gacita,* the legal newspaper, was final.

"Live in a Country of Fear and Silence"

VERN: From a perspective of some years, would you draw impressions as to the new government's actions vis-à-vis the religious sensitivity of Nicaraguans?

TERE: Religious instruction was never explicity forbidden. Nevertheless, the first problem was posed when Cuban teachers began to come into the country and were sent into small communities to help build schools. In a group raising a school wall, a Cuban might have overheard a Nicaraguan exclaim, "Thank God!"

In response, the Cuban might have retorted, "Thank God? That person doesn't exist! Don't thank God. Thank the state that gives you the material to build this school."

Nicaraguans began avoiding the Cubans when it became apparent what they were up to.

Publicly, we were told, "There is no condemnation of religion." However, incidents to the contrary were kept in full view.[1] Whenever there was a gathering, government-orientated individuals, though uninvited, were never far away. Once, when preparing to leave a charismatic assembly in which a Colombian priest had addressed three thousand people, we were informed that the Mob was outside. We were advised to be cautious.

A weekly newspaper called *La Semana Comica* is published in which all in authority who are thought of as being in opposition to the country's new leadership are ridiculed and made fun of. The church is especially featured along with Bishop Obando who was accused of being a Somocista, which he never was.

At this time I felt closer to other religious groups as long as they were Christian and believed in God.

VERN: When do you feel that the more open religious persecution began?

TERE: I would say it was in 1982, with the staged government attack upon Fr. Bismark Carballo, the Director of Catholic Radio which was later shut down by the government in 1985. A state agent who had made persistent requests for Fr. Carballo's counsel finally prevailed in obtaining an affirmative reply from him. With the Bishop's authorization, he went to her place for lunch. The police "happened" to be nearby when the lady's husband made a fuss.

What really happened? A government agent entered the lady's living quarter with a gun, had Fr. Carballo[2] undress and forced him outside into the arms of the state-controlled news media. Eventually, Fr. Carballo was expelled from Nicaragua and is now living in Miami.

VERN: How about your feelings toward a restoration of the refugees to Nicaragua?

TERE: There will be a return. Of course, I can't say when. The Left is so clever as it really outsmarts democratic societies. Nevertheless, we Nicaraguans believe that there is a reason why the Lord has allowed these things to happen and why Nicaragua was chosen to be the center of this whole conflict.

VERN: If the present government were dispossessed of its power, how do you feel new leaders should lead the nation?

TERE: Though most of us were not good practicing Catholics, our land is considered a Catholic country. We must live as Christians with Christ the Lord in mind and place Him before everything else. This is the only way we can prosper.

VERN: What have you heard recently from your home country?

TERE: I have received a number of letters. Among them was one from a priest and another from a nun. The nun emphasized the wonderful things which the Lord is doing. People are being converted to new life in the Lord despite the pressures.

The priest, who had been a professor, couldn't agree with his order which had sided with the government. He wasn't teaching anymore but was laboring hard in a rural church where he was fully aware of the persecution aimed at Christian workers.

He accompanied a young priest who had been summoned to a State Security office in one town. "I went with him just in case he might have been detained. I took him in my car."

My priest friend watched the fearsome drama passing in this "sinister office," as he called it. Individuals would enter very meekly, barely saying a word. Observing how afraid they were, he watched as they inquired of imprisoned relatives or brought in various parcels for them, some food or other necessity.

"We live in a country of fear and silence," he wrote. "All have become silent, afraid to speak out."

Enormous Communication, Little True Information

VERN: As you watched an entirely new group take over your nation, I heard something else. Was it true that "lovers of the Left" poured into Nicaragua from all over the globe? Refugees from remote rural areas exaggerated some to make their point that there were more foreigners in their nation than native Nicaraguans.

FRANK: These are known as internationalists. Most roam around more on a bumming, slumming campaign than anything else. Many, however, are the intellectuals who become advisors to the government. These were very evident in my work experience. Many times in negotiations there would be, say, ten advisors on the government side, two of these Nicaraguans and the rest foreigners.

Tere and I lived in a fairly well-to-do, secluded, and far-out section of Managua which included a number of embassies where these advisors began to occupy houses and former rental properties that had been "recuperated." Among them were Jesuits, other clergy and religious laymen, philosophers, economists, and state personnel from other countries.

The following examples of the names and numbers of embassy staff shed light on this topic: The Libyan mission includes over a thousand on their staff; the Russians count some four to five hundred on theirs; and the Bulgarians have over a hundred. At the diplomatic level, this small country of Nicaragua hosts something like five or six thousand Communist diplomats.[1]

VERN: Why the terrible inflation there?

FRANK: One of the things that always turns out to be a popped-up fly ball for Communists is the insidious slogan, "Revolution…for the worker." As the Left takes over, there is lots of organizing. Very soon it becomes evident that when there are two to supervise one, productivity decreases. Last year, Daniel Ortega denounced the farm worker as one who works three hours a day. If this is so, it would require almost three more days to equal the equivalent workday anywhere else.

Secondly, there occurs an enormous amount of pilferage.

Thirdly, there are the payments to other Communist nations such as Cuba.

Though the next point had been brought out earlier, it is the most important reason of all. It is necessary for the leaders of Nicaragua to have scarcity. Then they can have "Russian Rations." Rationed goods distributed by the government give authorities more political clout. This is what Communism is all about: "You don't do this or that, eh. Well, you won't get toilet paper!"

VERN: What worries you most concerning the U.S. political situation?

FRANK: I am worried that we're living in a world where there is an enormous amount of communication, but very little true information.

The Left in Central America want total power and will negotiate only to attain that. Left-wing individuals want power and don't care how many are killed just as long as they hold it in the end, to the detriment of freedom-loving humans, everywhere.[2]

To solve these problems, the United States requires statesmen who are willing to stake their jobs on justice for America, for those enslaved, and for those subjected to the lies of the Left. I don't doubt that ninety-nine percent of the leaders in Congress understand the Nicaraguan situation as well or even better than I, but most seem to be using the circumstances for their own personal and selfish benefit.

> The battle goes on for ending the freedoms represented in the U.S.A. But is it possible to rescue those under oppressive bondage in Cuba, Nicaragua, and other Latin American countries where Communist guerrillas control whole countrysides through drug dollars, such as in Colombia?[3]

Daisy Montiel Rodriguez and four of her five childen.

Daisy Montiel Rodriguez

Tegucigalpa, Honduras

December 18, 1986

> Intelligent, responsible, and sensitive, doing simple jobs to
> support her family under trying conditions, Daisy reveals
> a tenacity to be admired among "Those Passed By."

"Beautiful Country...Being Spoiled"

VERN: What happened to your husband?

DAISY: When the new government took over, it arrested him. He had been a chauffeur for Senator Pablo Rener de Valle from Puerto Cabezas and a civilian with para-military rank. He was charged with trafficking in arms or some such thing. Facing a twenty-three year imprisonment, somehow he was sentenced on a charge for three years.

VERN: Where did he spend his time?

DAISY: He was held at various places: El Chiptote in Managua, Carcel Modelo in Tipitapa, a certain prison in Chinandega, and then Zona Franca near Managua.[1]

VERN: Was he tortured?

DAISY: Several times…went through much. He really should speak for himself, but he gets upset when asked about the experience. I'll just mention a few things.

At Carcel Modelo, known as the "model prison" in Somoza's time, guards forced him to remain outside naked in the open air all night long. On the following day he was compelled to walk together with about thirty men, still naked, into a large room filled with military women. The prisoners were ordered to "show off," perform in a "pretty manner." Whoever refused was made to lie face down and a stick was pushed up his anus.

VERN: Under what circumstance did your husband leave Nicaragua?

DAISY: When his prison sentence ended in 1983, the government wanted him to work with State Security, but he refused. Whatever position he applied for, he would be turned down. In order to accomplish anything, I had to do the paperwork. Males have problems in Nicaragua!

In 1985 a summons came for his arrest.

VERN: What did he do then?

DAISY: He managed to secure a passport. After he left, our boy was the first of the children to go to Honduras. Then, the two oldest girls got out. All traveled by land.

VERN: Why were the children allowed to leave?

DAISY: Medical reasons.

VERN: Did the government wonder why the older children hadn't come back? What did it think about your husband?

DAISY: I said that my son was in Venezuela, and about my husband, I didn't know much. What I did know was that he had abandoned me for another woman and had gone to Panama.

Childen at play with women washing clothes below the
refugee camp at Teupasenti, El Paraiso, Honduras.

Agents searched my home and the CDS cut the government food source
for myself and the children. Officials got bored; I always gave them the same
answers.

VERN: When was your ration card taken away?

DAISY: When my husband went to Honduras. Every week there would be
harassment from the government, and I was forced to purchase more expen-
sively on the Black Market.

VERN: You were working all of this time?

DAISY: Yes.

VERN: What was your job?

DAISY: Until a few days ago, I was employed with INE, the Nicaraguan
Institute for Energy. Though I had been a longtime employee, my boss began
treating me in not such a nice way. He had found out that I was not getting
involved with the Block Committee, the CDS, where I lived and not doing
my revolutionary block guard duty. There developed a restructuring of our

work department and because he had been looking for an excuse to get rid of me, so he fired me.

I immediately went to the Office of Human Resources. The person in charge, along with the National Director of INE, ordered that I be returned to my old job.

VERN: How were things when you returned?

DAISY: I had been working at a man's job, chauffeuring various company-employed foreign men: French, Mexican and Italian. When the same boss began to accuse me of being a Contra, I decided to apply for work at IRENA, the Nicaraguan Insitute of National and Environmental Resources. After taking a special course, I was hired to do classification of lumber.

On the new job, someone recognized me and asked where my husband was. Because I replied, "He is in prison," the following day, I lost this new position.

Fortunately, with my return to INE, I got the old job back.

Another problem developed in that at the end of each workday, as I would be brought home in a government vehicle, the CDS took note of this and sent a letter of complaint stating that I had not been cooperating with the local CDS and that my husband was in prison.

My union, OTHINE (Organization of Workers of the Electrical Company of Nicaragua), took my side. With a baby to take care of, my reasons for not becoming involved with the CDS were legitimate.

VERN: How were your children treated in school?

DAISY: Before and after the new government takeover, everything went all right for my oldest children. They attended a former Somoza military school which had become a public school with its name changed to Rigoberto Lopez Perez.[2]

VERN: Where did your younger children study?

DAISY: The two younger girls studied at a school conducted by nuns.

VERN: Were your children taught anything concerning the Sandinista Communist emphasis?

DAISY: At the former military academy, yes. The subject came under the heading, "Civil Defense."

VERN: Children received this even in the lower grades?

DAISY: Yes, from the first to the fifth grades. Teachers taught the names and deeds connected with Sandinista political heroes.

VERN: Is there any sort of pressure placed upon the religious schools?

DAISY: Many religious schools do not accept government political indoctrination. Officials are planning to close these down.

VERN: When did this new emphasis come into being?

DAISY: About March of this year government officials began forcing religious schools to give equal time for religious and political themes. Many nuns did not accept this and planned to close their schools. Some of the following schools may disappear: Pureza de Maria, Divina Pastora, Annunciation School, Corazon de Maria, and Teresian Academy.[3] As the Ministry of Education is already sending instructors into religious schools to present the government point of view, it is certain that the Sandinistas will close those that stress religious teachings and exclude others that the party wants.

A requirement for graduation from high school forces students to go out to harvest cotton, coffee, sugar cane, etc. Anyone refusing is arrested. Once these young people are out in the rural areas and away from their parents, many immoral things take place. Returning home these young people tend to be disobedient and wild, with many girls having become pregnant. The end result is that a whole mess of trouble is cultivated in Nicaragua.

The government has even required girls from thirteen to nineteen to be out fighting in the mountains, where there are two battalions of them.

VERN: Did you and your husband belong to a church?

DAISY: Catholic.

VERN: What sort of association did you notice between the church and the governmental political emphasis?

DAISY: Our family used to belong to a church called St. Mary of the Angels [Santa Maria de los Angeles] in Managua. The priest of the church, a Franciscan, Uriel Molina from Matagalpa, stressed things in a half-and-half manner, half politics and half church teaching.

VERN: Is he still there?

DAISY: Yes, he is…he goes around armed and travels in one of three government vehicles stuffed with bodyguards.

The church building used to have pictures and paintings of saints. These have been replaced with photos of Rigoberto, Sandino, Carlos Fonseca, etc.

VERN: When did you first belong to this congregation?

DAISY: I got married there but left it fourteen years ago. No one attends the church's Mass, more politics than anything else, unless a person takes sides with Sandinista political philosophy.

VERN: Where did you worship next?

DAISY: A couple of other churches in Managua. Each was in the area where I lived. Later, moving back to the vicinity of St. Mary of the Angels, I attended but only one more time. Hearing the priest emphasizing that one should make scarves and flags with Sandinista slogans and colors, I never returned.

VERN: How did you finally get out?

DAISY: I had a health reason and also succeeded in getting permits to travel with my two remaining girls. Asked by officials how I was able to secure the finances for air tickets, I responded by saying, "An aunt from the United States sent them."

VERN: How did the departure go?

DAISY: There were some tense moments. My exit permit was to expire on the eighteenth of this month, today! So, going to the airport for the departure on the sixteenth, I was informed that an Argentine visa was required.

VERN: Why an Argentine visa?

DAISY: I don't know, but this was no time to argue. I got it!

Back at the airport, informed this time that I had to have a round trip ticket, a friend loaned me the money.

Manuel Jiron Castrillo with his son, Manuel, assisting with the newly published book, *Quien es quien en Nicaragua.*

Manuel Jiron

Tegucigalpa, Honduras

January 30, 1987

When students protested during the House Un-American Activities Committee hearings in San Francisco in the 1950s and into 1960, it was the Communists who took control of the demonstrations.[1] Manuel Jiron Castrillo demon strated for more freedom. Guess who benefited in the end?

"Mystique…Charisma…Charm"

MANUEL: I am Manuel Jiron, who for thirty years in Nicaragua worked conscientiously in my profession as an Impressario and Director of Radio

Broadcasting. A specialist in Media and Mass Communication, I directed and owned radio stations.

During the insurrection against the Somozas, I was among those following the Popular Support[2] ideology and not among the Sandinista Front, which was in the vanguard of the action. I fought openly against Somoza and saw my broadcasting stations destroyed by the National Guard. In September 1978, I fled to the Panamanian Embassy in Managua. From there I went into Costa Rican exile in November of the same year where I continued the fight by running the clandestine Radio Sandino.

After the triumph of the people over Somoza, I returned to Nicaragua. I want to emphasize that the victory came as the result of citizens' actions and not solely because of Sandinista Front or Party involvement. The struggle by the people had been for liberty, but the new government, the Sandinista Party, did not grant it.[3]

I criticized what was happening and began to fight against the ugliness that was being placed on Nicaraguans. I managed to participate in this battle within Nicaragua for no more than two years.

On two occasions after rebuilding my broadcasting facilities, the stations' transmissions were jammed by the new authorities. In December 1980, the government-supported Divine Mobs damaged the property and came back in March 1981 to do the final destruction.

Public liberties disappeared completely, along with fifty-seven daily radio stations. Two television stations were stolen. One of the most important newspaper businesses[4] was confiscated and utilized by the FSLN party.

The daily free press of Nicaragua[5] is closed permanently. This is something which the Somoza regime had not done in its forty-seven years of control as it at least permitted a middle ground of liberty and never closed daily presses nor radio stations.

VERN: Wasn't Somoza a little hard on *La Prensa*?

MANUEL: There was the rare occasion for *La Prensa* when he felt that it had gone too far within his sense of fair play. Yes, he submitted the radio stations to some repressive laws of censorship. Political liberties were permitted to some extent, but Somoza never persecuted the religious of the country.

The Sandinistas have. This has been done to Catholics, Protestants, and whatever. As Marxism-Leninism considers religion the "opiate of the people," the government has expelled a number of Catholic clergy in spite of the fact that the vast majority of the nation is Catholic.

VERN: How do you consider the United States' stance, including that of its press, touching the Central American issues?

MANUEL: Consciously or unconsciously, I believe the North American press is playing the game of international Communism. Both the *New York Times* and the *Washington Post* are on the side against what President Reagan desires for Central America.

While the U.S. continues to experience liberty and democracy, it takes one year for its Congress to decide if it is going to allow the hundred million dollars to be given to the Contras. As I see it, the Contras already have gotten the message of what the United States is saying: "Don't gain the victory! Don't win!" While the Sandinistas were receiving heavy military armaments, special helicopters, tanks, and all that is necessary for war, the United States does not supply the Contras with proper equipment.[6]

It appears that the fight for liberty is weaker than the Sandinista forces who are duping the world that their present Nicaraguan governing methods promote democracy.

When Russia was brought up in Latin America fifteen years ago, it was as if one were speaking of the moon. Now it all comes down to this: countries in Central America believe Russia is a better ally and friend than the United States.[7]

VERN: Would you give details of your background?

MANUEL: I was born into a middle-class family in south Nicaragua in 1936, with my middle years spent in the nation's capital. I studied broadcasting and was trained as an orator and public speaker.

I went to Mexico when I was chosen to act in a biography of Jose Mojica, a Mexican actor who had taken vows in the Franciscan order. It was quite an experience to see my name placed upon theater marquees with with the famous artists of the Mexican film industry.

Further study in Dramatic Arts and Merchandising occupied my attention until returning to Nicaragua where I was placed in charge of three radio stations, all having low ratings, namely sixteenth, eighteenth, and twentieth places. In a very short interval of time, these rose to be among the commercial leaders in the land.

Later, I was employed by Pedro Joaquin Chamorro Cardenal,[8] Director and Editor of the daily newspaper, *La Prensa,* and served as the Director of Radio Centauro.

In 1970 I founded my own radio stations, Mi Preferida and Radio Amor. Mi Preferida rose very rapidly to be the leading commercial radio station replacing one that had occupied that position for twenty-five years.

The new business was lucrative, bringing with it some financial power. Because of this, I was able to get involved in politics in 1976. But then, Somoza began repressions against me. As I was not permitted to give political announcements on radio, the only avenue open for me was the one I took. I fled the country.

Tired of the Somoza rule and elated by the thought of ousting a family monopoly, we were attracted by the new mystique, charisma, and charm of the Sandinistas.

Returning to Nicaragua[9] only to be exiled again, I feel as if my forced exile already has been too long. However, I've tried to make the best of it. I have published six books including the one that I am now promoting in Honduras. It's entitled, *Quien es Quien en Nicaragua*[10], "Who's Who in Nicaragua," and has become a bestseller in Costa Rica and Panama.

Frequently, I write for the *Nacion, La Republic,* and *La Prensa,* the three most influential newspapers in Costa Rica, and, I might add, in all of Central America. I also write in *Aria Prensa* (Area Press) in Panama and some of my articles are printed in the Miami *Herald.*

It was impossible for me to take any of my assets out of Nicaragua. I was privileged to have the opportunity to start a small business in Costa

Rica, where I sell musical records, tapes, and accessories for radio and communication equipment.

VERN: How many children do you have?

MANUEL: Six girls, three in university training and three not yet there, and Manuel who is thirteen.

Takeover Montage

VERN: Give a few glimpses of the Sandinista takeover.

Manuel: Who is it that has been giving aid to further Sandinista dominance in the oppressing of its Nicaraguan citizens as well as posing a grave danger for other countries in North and South America? None other than the United Nations, which is composed of 173 countries, with its major portion leaning to the political Left and supporting the Sandinista Front.[1]

When Somoza governed Nicaragua's people in a questionable manner, the Organization of American States[2] pressured him to abandon the nation and its people. Toward a more irresponsible government such as the Sandinistas, the same standards were not applied.

Because Contadora[3] manages nothing more than to consolidate the Sandinista Front, which considers Contadora weak, the Sandinista hold on Nicaragua probably will not be toppled.

My discernment and experience as a Christian lead me to conclude that the only way to free the enslaved people of Nicaragua is through armed struggle.

VERN: Who are the Contras?

MANUEL: The Contras are constituted as a local, regional, and nationalist organization. They are a partner in the goals of the U.S. and should be considered as such. But it appears as if the Contras serve for some American leadership as a convenient scapegoat for these same leaders' lack of courage as to how to defend their part of the world.

The Contras are not mercenaries. They are Nicaraguan youth along with older men and women who have given themselves in the fight for freedom. They live on no more than bare subsistence with very little food, only the daily necessities.[4]

As I understand that a mercenary is one who is given compensation for doing something in a conflict within a country not his own. There are, indeed, mercenaries in this civil war in Nicaragua, the more than 20,000 foreign internationalists, employed by the Sandinistas to promote the Communist takeover of my country.[5]

VERN: How about the question of aid to the Contras?

MANUEL: Freedom fighters are those who work without expecting to receive pay. However, it is important for the Contras and their support units to receive family allotment support. The majority of the Contras are not receiving adequate family assistance.

In contrast, the foreign mercenaries under the Sandinista government receive a great amount of remuneration for being in Nicaragua for the purpose of oppressing and subverting its population.

VERN: What do you know of religious persecution by the government in Nicaragua?

MANUEL: As they are materialists, Sandinista Party members repress all that is spiritual in a great effort to divide Christian churches. The Communists have promoted such men as Ernesto and Fernando Cardenal, Miguel D'Escoto Brockman and Edgard Parrales[6,] religiously trained individuals who are really Leftists.

Preaching in a Popular Church sanctuary with the world press covering the event, Daniel Ortega declared, "Reagan is a criminal!"

Government disdain for genuine Nicaraguan religious life occurred when Pope John Paul II arrived in the country in 1983. Government supported Divine Mobs and members of the Popular Church staged a deliberate disturbance.

A very lamentable history has been that of the Sandinista persecution of the Miskito Indians, who are Christian. Though there were very few foreign pastors among them, these were accused by the government of being imperialists and promoters of the CIA against Nicaraguan authorities.

The latest civil rights abuses which the Christian Church has suffered include, in 1985, pressure to close official publishing facilities of the Catholic Church in Managua. A few months later in 1986, Catholic Radio was involuntarily shut down. In June 1986, Monsignor Bismark Carballo, the Director of Catholic Radio and the Secretary for Cardinal and Archbishop Miguel Obando Bravo, was expelled. Bishop Pablo Antonio Vega was also exiled a short time later in July.[7]

VERN: Would you relate more as to your flight from Nicaragua, the second time?

MANUEL: I am very critical in the promotion of my political strategy. I became convinced that I could not remain in Nicaragua. If I did, the only reaction that reasonably could be expected from the Sandinistas was the printing of my death notice.

Because we Nicaraguans have not been strong enough to unite in our striving for liberty and freedom, it is my belief that I must participate in this task. God will assist the people of the democratic world in helping us obtain the liberation of our homeland and aid us in the strengthening of the democracies in our area.

VERN: When did you discover that you had made a mistake in associating with the Sandinistas?

MANUEL: A good question! As I was considered a part of the infrastructure with Sandinista leadership, I was present when they were discussing their policies of participating with other groups that wanted a united, pluralistic political front for Nicaragua after an expected victory over Somoza. As the Popular Support groups were urging the permitting of many liberties including the freedom of expression, Daniel Ortega didn't want to sign the document that had been prepared. Fellow Sandinista members told him that the document was not that important because they were now in control. They encouraged him to sign, so their work could be done that much more effectively.

As a result of this meeting held in a house behind the Catholic Clinic in San Jose, Costa Rica, in 1979, the groundwork for the "Pacto Puntare-nas"[8] was signed.

A few days later during a conversation of the Directorate,[9] I was told that when the Sandinistas triumphed, they would allow only certain mediums of communication.

This news provided all the persuasion that I needed to oppose the Sandinistas. I protested immediately.

Salvador Montenegro

Tegucigalpa, Honduras

June 23, 1987

Insights from Shrewd Business Acumen

"Neither a Dictator nor a Democrat"

SALVADOR: My father was the National Guard Commander in Bluefields, where I was born in 1936. Six months later, my parents moved to Managua where I was raised and where my father's side of the family traces its history back two centuries.

Educated at the University of Michigan and the University of Tennessee, I remained in the United States from 1954 to 1963. Returning to Nicaragua, I was employed as a professional in business until I fled in 1979.

VERN: When in '79?

SALVADOR: Twenty-two days before the Sandinista takeover.

VERN: You already knew what they were like?

SALVADOR: Definitely. They never said anything else to the contrary. They always told the people that they were Marxist-Leninists.

VERN: Why didn't Nicaraguans realize this?

SALVADOR: They wanted to get rid of Somoza.

VERN: How long did your father remain in army work?

SALVADOR: He left the army with the rank of captain in 1944. He died in 1972.

VERN: Would you give a little political background information on the Somoza family?

SALVADOR: In the 1926 Revolution, the Liberal Party was defeating government forces led by the Conservative Party.[1] All fighting stopped when the United States forced free elections upon the country and Jose Maria Moncada, a Liberal, was elected president in 1928. The U.S. also hand-picked another Liberal, Anastasio Somoza Garcia, to head the newly formed Nicaraguan National Guard.

After Moncada's legal tenure in office, another Liberal, Dr. Juan Bautista Sacasa, was elected in a popular vote. Anastasio Somoza Garcia overthrew him and became president in 1937 according to Nicaraguan Law. He was re-elected in 1939. When his tenure ended, Somoza hand-picked Victor Roman, who was elected in 1944. Roman had been in office only about two and a half years when Somoza again returned to the presidency. With the assassination of Anastasio Somoza in 1956, his son Luis took over and, in turn, was elected president and remained in office until 1963, when Rene Schick Gutierrez, another hand-picked man, was elected. Schick died in office and was succeeded by Lorenzo Guerrero Gutierrez, who held office until 1967, when Anastasia Somoza Debayle took over the position.

When the president's term ended in 1972, a junta was formed by three men: two from the ruling Liberal Party and one from the Conservative Party. This junta ended the same year the earthquake struck, and Anastasio Somoza Debayle took the reins of leadership again. In 1974, when the term of office was extended to six years, he was re-elected.

VERN: Even though some have quoted a greater number of years, Anastasia Somoza Garcia took over in 1937 in a formal way and the family rule lasted for forty-two years, even with other names in the office of presidency.

SALVADOR: If no one within the family was in the presidency, the family was the actual power behind the position.

VERN: Would you tell something of your business experience in Nicaragua?

SALVADOR: In 1963 I began as the Office Manager for the Colgate-Palmolive Company. From 1967 to 1979, I became associated with the largest beer brewery, Compania Servicio de Nicaragua, and served as its Marketing Manager.

VERN: There are those who say that when companies were begun in Nicaragua, Somoza would exact fifty percent of the profits. Is there anything to such allegations?

SALVADOR: This is not true at all. He had his own companies, companies with partners, and invested in others as is the practice in the United States. Companies were started every day in Nicaragua, and it would have been impossible for Somoza to demand fifty percent of all the profits. He was being talked about in an untruthful way.

VERN: What percent of the companies in Nicaragua did Somoza own?

SALVADOR: This is impossible to say. He had his own big ones, such as the airline company, the shipping company, and a bank. Then, toward the end of his rule, he went into some large ranch holdings, a sugar mill, auto dealerships, etc.

There were many, many more privately owned businesses within Nicaragua which disprove those charges against Somoza. Though I would say that he was the richest man in the country, one cannot say that he owned even ten percent of the country's wealth.

VERN: The Left has done their work very well in spreading propaganda to local people in Nicaragua, to say nothing about teachers in American universities. I heard a well-educated United States citizen state that Somoza owned half of the good farmland.

SALVADOR: This is from a completely misinformed person.

VERN: Did you know any of the present Sandinista leaders?

SALVADOR: I knew most of them. As a matter of fact, though some of them worked with or for me for a while, I didn't know that they were Sandinistas.

Rodrigo Reyes, who is the the Sandinista Minister of Justice in Nicaragua, worked for an advertising company that we had with the brewery.

VERN: Was he a lawyer?

SALVADOR: Studying to become one; he was an Account Supervisor at the office.

VERN: Why didn't Somoza leave earlier?

SALVADOR: He didn't have very good advisors. He was a very stubborn and powerful man, and many were afraid of him, afraid of telling the truth.

VERN: Did you know any of these advisors, personally?

SALVADOR: Oh yes, very, very closely. Some claimed that they talked with him, privately, about this matter, but never publicly.

VERN: Did you, yourself, know him?

SALVADOR: Yes.

VERN: What was he like?

SALVADOR: Very intelligent and knowledgeable. He was a very bad dictator because he was trying to be a democrat. Although he was too soft to be a dictator, many believed that he couldn't be a democrat because he had been in power for such a long time. Let's just say that he was a bad dictator and a terrible democrat, or that he was neither a dictator nor a democrat.

VERN: It's unfortunate that he didn't give up sooner in favor of other leadership. Apparently he thought that he was doing good for Nicaragua.

SALVADOR: He thought that he was the Savior of Nicaragua. Knowing that the Sandinistas were Communists, he didn't want to leave the country in their hands. This he told everybody.

VERN: Do you think that if he would have left earlier, Nicaragua would have had a chance?

SALVADOR: Definitely! If he had done this after his heart attack in 1977, the nation would have had the opportunity to survive. If he had requested a national government representing the different political tendencies, things would be different today.

VERN: National Guard officers have been accused of being involved in graft. Were they participants?

SALVADOR: Yes, however, the average guardsman was not involved in anything such as this. He just did his work for the small pay he received.

Those who shared in graft were in the upper echelons, the colonels and the generals. Those, say, from captain and below did not have the opportunity.

VERN: The National Guardsmen were and are, even to this day, used as scapegoats in covering Sandinista crimes. One important person in these policies is Tomas Borge. Did you know him?

SALVADOR: No, I only knew of him. His life was pardoned two or three times by the Somozas.[2]

VERN: Getting back to the subject of graft within the National Guard, would you say that Somoza himself permitted this?

SALVADOR: Yeah, he knew about it.

VERN: Is this attitude typical of the Central American area?

SALVADOR: I hear of this all over the world, and wouldn't say it only happens in Central America.

VERN: Would you say that Somoza was a participant in some of the graft?

SALVADOR: Yes. But as I have said, Nicaraguans were tired of the Somoza name. Also, there was another problem. Somoza's son was becoming too powerful. It was known that after the present Somoza, there would be another.[3] Those who wanted this dynasty to stop were encouraged by businessmen who thought commerce, education, etc. would then improve.

VERN: Is it true to say that when one takes stock of the different forces which were fighting Somoza, the campesinos weren't a part of this?

SALVADOR: They were living happily with their own crop planting: coffee, corn, rice, etc. With enough for them to eat and education slowly improving, everything was working fairly well.[4]

VERN: Things were getting better, slowly.

SALVADOR: Slowly, but things were getting better. There was no hunger in Nicaragua.

Cause of Somoza's Fall

VERN: Could it be said that it was the middle class that caused the downfall of the Somoza government?

SALVADOR: Not only the middle class. It was also foreign governments who tied Somoza's hands so that he couldn't defend himself. I understand that Mr. Carter began his campaign about human rights, pointed his finger at Somoza, and that was it. When the United States decides to overthrow somebody, when it really decides, it does it.

VERN: Do you think that civil rights were abused in Nicaragua?

SALVADOR: I believe that during the war, there were abuses when the struggle was taking place between the government and the Sandinistas. But where is the line drawn for abuses while a civil war is raging? When someone is trying to kill another, those battling will defend themselves.

VERN: Did President Carter and his advisors think that if Somoza were out of the way, a better situation would evolve?

SALVADOR: They probably thought so. I don't know why. They didn't know the Sandinistas, I guess.[1]

The Sandinistas didn't have a party. Some of them were just plain bandits. Some didn't like any sort of government. I believe that some were idealists, but very few. All hinged on having a Communist government.

VERN: Opposition parties existed in Somoza's time?

SALVADOR: Totally. They did whatever they wanted to do.

VERN: He always was successful in winning elections.

SALVADOR: People were not unhappy. They were not forced to vote. When certain parties decided not to go for elections, those of the electorate who would have voted for these parties went to the polls and cast their ballots for Somoza. People could express themselves. There were the Freedoms of the Press and Religion. Citizens were free to do anything they wanted to do. A person could go into the street and yell, "Down with Somoza," and nobody would say anything. This happened every day.

VERN: I have read that just before his overthrow, Somoza could rally seventy-five thousand Nicaraguans to a political meeting.[2]

SALVADOR: He did. People went to his rally because they wanted to go. The cordobas in his time were equal to seven for one U.S. dollar. Today, the rate is seven thousand to one.

VERN: Why did the people like Somoza?

SALVADOR: He was charismatic and knew the language. Besides, Nicaragua was progressing every year. While the exports amounted to seven million dollars in 1941, they went to something like eight hundred million in 1974 or 1975. Progress in a very poor country had been improving and someone in government was managing this ship very well.[3]

VERN: On these issues United States news media has tended to lean in the direction of the Left .

SALVADOR: One can see it every day.

President Reagan has done more for the United States than any other president within the last forty years. Internationally, the Democrats have been trying to keep him from doing anything. Inflation, interest, and unemployment are down. What does a nation want from a president? Now the Democrats are trying to impeach him for the Iran-Contra affair. I don't understand some of the politicians in the United States. Mr. Reagan has been the best president I've seen in my lifetime.

VERN: When you felt forced to leave Nicaragua, did you come to Honduras?

SALVADOR: No, I went to Miami. About a year ago, I came to Honduras.

VERN: There certainly seems to be more stability here because of the United States presence.

SALVADOR: Nicaraguan leaders say of themselves that they have an expansionist policy. They have stated many times that they want to expand.

If the United States left Honduras, we all would have to leave because the Sandinistas would take it over with the backing of the Cubans and the Soviet Union. There would be no way in which Nicaragua could be stopped, other than by the States.

VERN: There have been charges that certain leaders have mishandled money among the Freedom Fighters.

SALVADOR: Maybe, Freedom Fighter political leaders are not doing as good a job as its military leaders, but it is very difficult for its political leadership to live in poverty in such locations as Miami or Costa Rica. There needs to be a house, a car, food, security, and certain other facilities. Time will take care of everything in regard to this.

In the meanwhile, those who deserve our recognition and support are the Freedom Fighters who are fighting within Nicaragua. One such person I take pride in singling out among the thousands is Bermudez,[4] the FDN Commander. For many years he has been a man on the front.

VERN: He has been accused by the Sandinistas and the Left within the United States as an example of the crooked former National Guard that leads the Contras.

SALVADOR: I know this man and have known him since he was a Lieu-tenant in the late '50s. In step with his own merits, he has not been cor-rupted but is a true leader, a true patriot. Bermudez never was in a position in Nicaragua where he could have been a corrupted official. During Somoza's ouster, he was in Washington, D.C., as the Nicaraguan Military Attaché.

As the Sandinistas run a regime of terror, Freedom Fighters need more aid from the United States and its armed forces.

I admire the Freedom Fighters and support them, but I am not a part of any of their directorship, and do not know what the combatants are doing. This I know, however; they are fighting and deserve all of my respect.

Pastor Ricardo Duarte

Tegucigalpa, Honduras

July 11, 1987

> Nicaragua could be compared to the state of Iowa in reference to area and population. However, the populations of Cedar Rapids, Council Bluffs, Des Moines, Dubuque, and Waterloo must be brought to zero to conservatively dramatize how many Nicaraguan citizens have fled.

Life's Prelude

RICARDO: On April 3, 1953, I was born in the Nicaraguan village of Capire near Las Trojes, Honduras. Since that time, by force of a treaty, this village of my birth was taken back as a part of Honduran territory.

VERN: I would be honored if you would relate the full story as to why you are not now living in Nicaragua.

RICARDO: At eleven years of age, I moved to an uncle's home in the city of Jinotega, Nicaragua, where I began to smoke and drink. When my uncle died and as I was on my own, I traveled to Managua where I immediately began taking drugs. A year later, I became involved in the occult and homosexual practices were added to my list of vices in order to purchase drugs.

VERN: What sort of drugs were you taking?

RICARDO: Marijuana, LSD, glue sniffing, hallucinatory mushrooms, and smoking or drinking as tea certain other hallucinatory plants, both the white and red varieties.

I began to see horrible and ugly faces laughing at me after being in the occult for about six months. The mental concentration practices of this occult group didn't help. While trying to sleep, these faces became very real to me,and I found myself going insane.

One day in November 1968, at seven o'clock in the morning, I boarded a train and got off at the first stop, La Curbade, south of Managua's airport.[1] Then, after walking some fifteen minutes and passing many houses, I stopped at one which turned out to be the home of a Pentecostal pastor, Manuel Veliz, and his wife, Louisa. They belonged to a Christian group known as the Prince of Peace Church. Both Manuel and Louisa were sixty-eight years of age.

Of course, it was all in the perfect will of God. It was now around eight o'clock as I walked up to the entrance and this couple was standing there. The man asked me what I wanted. I answered that I was looking for a job.

After the pastor turned to his wife, asked her to pray to God and inquire what sort of a boy Ricardo was, they both began to pray and speak in tongues.

VERN: You were listening to this?

RICARDO: Yes, I thought that they were praying in a foreign language which they knew and preferred rather than Spanish.

VERN: And the decision?

RICARDO: The pastor's wife answered that God had sent this boy to their house for help. They invited me into their home.

VERN: How many belonged to the pastor's congregation?

RICARDO: About 130 members.

VERN: Were you impressed by this church?

RICARDO: I saw and heard things at their services which I never had experienced before. When I heard preaching concerning the Blood of Christ, I became very frightened.

On January 1, 1969, while under the influence of drugs and perched high above the pastor's house, I was trimming a tree in preparation for cutting it down. While swinging a machete, I fell 150 feet to the ground.

I was taken to a public charity hospital. Though I was paralyzed from my waist down for most of a month's stay, I felt that I'd be able to walk again. But on the 28th day when a doctor informed me of the opposite fact, I became desperate. While calling upon God for help, I thought of suicide. If I'd had a gun, I would have killed myself.

Back at the pastor's home, the pastor along with other pastors said that I would be able to walk again. After a month I accepted Jesus.

Pastor Ricardo Duarte. his wife (the former Felipa de Jesus Mejia), and daughters..

One afternoon about two months later, while praying alone for God to aid me, I added that it didn't matter if I would not be able to walk in the manner in which I had been used to doing. I prayed that if He would heal me, I would serve Him in a full-time way. Boldly, I then said, "In the name of Jesus, I can stand up."

All of a sudden, a fire came upon my head, I started to speak in tongues, my bones began to crack including those in the paralyzed areas, and I felt a warmth all over. Forced upward from the wheelchair and unto the floor, I began walking and dancing.

Brethren began coming to the pastor's house. Both the pastor and his wife knew that God had performed a miracle.

Though there remained some stiffness within the fingers of my left hand, my left ankle and toes, and toes on my right foot, I was able to get up and walk. I feel God left these symptoms as a testimony that real healing had been accomplished.

Within a month after the healing, I left Pastor Veliz's home and did some traveling. About six months later I was baptized after a period of instruction in God's Word.

I moved to Yali in the state of Jinotega where I got lodging with a pastor of the Assembly of God Church. Here I met the Mejia family along with their daughter, Felipa de Jesus Mejia, whom I married a year later.

In Managua I became the pastor of an Assembly of God Church in the barrio of La Concepcion and, after a year, I began serving a church in San Bartolo in the state of Managua, remaining there for fourteen months.

As is the custom of the Assembly of God churches, pastors are moved within short periods of time from one church to another. Thus followed service at Jalapa, LaPaz-Murra, Siapala, all in Nueva Segovia, and at Wambán in Jinotega.

Because of my wife's health, I was forced to leave this church and move to her parent's home in Murra. While there, the brethren of La Paz-Murra who lived some ten kilometers north of Murra wanted me to become their pastor again. As the church at Wambán had gotten a new pastor, I accepted the new call.

A Mission

RICARDO: The La Paz-Murra congregation began to fast and pray during the middle of 1980. It continued to do so for seven months when, at the end of that time, the Lord spoke to them through prophetic utterance that a persecution would be coming over churches in Nicaragua. They were moved by the Lord to spread this message throughout the whole nation of Nicaragua.

VERN: What was the size of the church membership?

RICARDO: One hundred sixty from age fourteen.

VERN: Who conveyed this message to the country?

RICARDO: Twelve people. There were four sisters and eight brothers which included myself.

We started this labor beginning in the month of February of 1981. The group was still traveling when I was arrested for the first time on January 4, 1982. The Sandinistas found out what we were doing.

VERN: Where and how were you arrested?

RICARDO: Our La Paz-Murra congregation was conducting a spiritual retreat which had been in progress for two days. Each day the meeting began at 7:00 A.M. and continued without stopping till 7:00 P.M.

Eight State Security policemen, dressed in civilian clothing and armed with AK-47 Soviet rifles, interrupted our meeting at around two o'clock in the afternoon and took me to the jail in Murra.

Interrogation was done within four days by one person at night from eleven o'clock for as long as six hours each time. Not counting the questioning, no torture was used.

Sandinistas thought of our church members as Contras. Likewise, the whole village was so labeled. Our Assembly of God Church was the only one in the community.

One Sunday morning at approximately ten o'clock when the church was assembled with about seventy members who were with their children at worship services, the La Paz-Murra Church was terrorized, along with the whole village. Mortar shells were exploded, machine guns were fired, and grenades were set off. Adults and children were knocked from their seats by the exploding concussions. The church's ceiling and roof were damaged, and a few houses in the small community were destroyed.

In all of this, only one person was injured. It happened to be one of the fourteen-year-old girls who had received the prophetic message. During the shelling, she fell and cut her head. No one else in the village became a casualty, as many happened to be gone that morning.

This incident occurred at the time of the beginning of persecution of Christians throughout the whole of Nicaragua including the states of Nueva Segovia, Jinotega, Esteli, Matagalpa, etc. Pastors were also killed.

VERN: Let's get the date.

RICARDO: January 1982. Four months later I was arrested, again.

VERN: Why was this?

RICARDO: My church and I didn't obey the order of the authorities of the state to stop traveling and preaching as we were doing. My second arrest occurred in May.

VERN: Would you go into detail?

RICARDO: I was taken off the street by fourteen men dressed in the uniform of the Popular Militia, all armed with the AK-47s. I was placed in a small Toyota car with four men. We were accompanied by an army truck carrying the other soldiers.

On this occasion I was taken to Jicaro, a town larger than Murra on the road to Ocotal .

I was brought to a special office for two sessions, each beginning around twelve midnight and lasting from two to three hours. I had to face one of two interrogators, Campanerio and Flaco. If I didn't answer a question, they would hit me with an iron bar.

I was asked about the other church members who were spreading God's message throughout Nicaragua and ordered to stop it. They wanted to know why I was not allowing church members to attend the public Sandinista meetings where they'd get information from the Militia and the CDS.

VERN: What was the confinement like?

RICARDO: Except for interrogation, I was kept in solitary confinement. The cell had a dirt floor and I was forced to sleep on it with its filth, insects, and mosquitoes. There was no window except for the iron bars of the door.

VERN: Were you called by any names?

RICARDO: The words, "Little Pastor," were used as I stood about five-feet-five and weighed about 115 pounds.

VERN: How long were you there?

RICARDO: Ten days.

VERN: What happened when you were set free?

RICARDO: As the church fasted and prayed, the Lord told us that we would be allowed to leave the country in the future. In the meanwhile, our ministry throughout Nicaragua was to continue.

Mission Price Increase

RICARDO: When the Sandinistas realized that they could not halt the spiritual movement of our congregation, they arrested me for the third time on December 11, 1982.

I left my home at about eight o'clock in the morning to visit to a brother and came upon a group of some sixty-five soldiers. How they knew where I'd be was probably due to the work of spies which we had inside the congregation. Under a Communist government, nothing can be done to get rid of them.

The one with the pseudonym Flaco, meaning "Thin One," was there. He was Chief of State Security over the area of Murra, Jicaro, and Quilali. He taunted me, "So you are the famous pastor in this area. Oh, damned pastor! Your fame is now finished. But talk to your God." He added as an afterthought, "Maybe, He also can talk to the gringos?"

VERN: Had any gringo[1] ever helped you?

RICARDO: No. Knowing that I had been traveling to many places in Nicaragua, the officer informed me that the gringos had brainwashed me.

I replied that it was not they who had washed my brain, but the Blood of Christ.

With this exchange, Flaco went from in front of me to my back, hit me with the barrel of his AK-47, kicked me with his boots, and socked me with a fist while the whole troop of soldiers laughed.

VERN: Would you estimate their ages?

RICARDO: Sixteen to thirty.

Among them was a very tall, blond, weighing two hundred pounds or so, also in uniform. He did not speak and seemed to be a foreigner.

Early the following morning at about one o'clock, I was taken out of a Murra jail cell. Then, after being transported south of Murra, I was led about sixty feet into an abandoned mine shaft where I expected to be shot. It turned out to be an interrogation.

The morning's experience was repeated seven more times at the same location with different persons doing the questioning. Each session lasted two hours.

VERN: Why did your captors take you to this tunnel?

RICARDO: The Sandinistas preferred to keep the proceedings as secretive as possible.

VERN: What about the cell conditions at Murra?

RICARDO: Food, water, and a blanket were brought to me from the brethren. All prisoners had a mat to sleep on.

Taken to Jicaro by Flaco and Campanerio who were in the front seat, I was forced to lie face down on the floor in the back of the vehicle with my hands tied at my back. The ride took about an hour.

In the new location, the question was put to me, "Are you going to talk?" Campanerio added that any Christian pastor who did not agree with the Revolution would be caused to disappear. While being interrogated, I was kicked, hit in the chest with a small iron bar, instructed not to ever reveal

Country scene south of Teupasent, El Paraiso, Honduras.

Children at the Guasimos camp, Jacaleapa, El Paraiso, Honduras.

to anyone what was happening to me, and placed in solitary confinement for ten days.

Three pastors came to the jail and left juice for me to drink, but Flaco took it away and didn't allow me to have any.

At the end of these days, at about midnight, I was placed in a Jeep with dark-tinted glass. In the front were the same Flaco and Campanerio,[2] who was driving. In the back, four soldiers placed their feet upon me. One had his feet upon my head. Some even kicked me.

After this trip of an hour I was taken to the jail at Quilali, a town larger than Jicaro. Here one of the soldiers who had been sitting in the back seat announced to the new jailers, "Look, we are bringing the famous 'Little Pastor' from La Paz."

The soldiers shoved me so forcefully ino the cell that my weak body hit the opposite wall. I fell to the floor, where I lay for an hour before getting up.

With all of my clothes taken away, I was ordered to lie down in a large, dry pine coffin situated on the floor. It was supposed to be the one which would be holding me when I died. Alone in this cell of about eight by ten feet and with the floor made of cement, it was not difficult to understand that the coffin would serve as the best place to sleep.

At about four AM, I was taken to a tiny space, maybe three by three feet, given a name list of pastors and asked to make accusations of actions against the Sandinista government. I was told that if I would not do this, my wife andfamily would be killed.

The two green-uniformed State Security men now questioning me were called the Furious One of the North and the Vulture. I told the Furious One that anyone who was a liar would not be allowed to enter heaven. I would not tell lies to save myself.

Back in my jail cell, the Vulture placed a knife to my throat and threat-ened to kill if I did not do what they wanted. As I did not answer, I was forced to stand on my left foot for about eight hours. If my right foot touched the floor, I was hit with a rifle barrel, which happened roughly five times.

A portion of dwellings at Guasimos refugee camp, Jacaleapa, El Paraiso, Honduras.

Washing clothes below the Teupasenti refugee camp.

Now the starting time was between midnight and two in the morning. Each session would last up to five hours. Because I refused to go along with what my jailers wanted, they would tie my hands, hang me by my feet, and swing me like a top while firing questions at me.

This torture was administered about nine times. After each of these sessions, I was brought back to the cell with the coffin. I was allowed to go to the toilet but was forced to walk the 120 feet with my head down by my knees.

At the end of eighteen days, I was transferred to Ocotal, where I was kept for four days but not questioned.

I spent eleven days at La Barranca, an underground jail. I was dealt with by a broad-shouldered, black Cuban who emphasized that I was going to talk.

I was forced to bend over a pool of water that stood a few feet above the floor and my head was submerged with the words that this "exercise" would "refresh" my memory. The Cuban ordered, "Tell me! Among the pastors, are there many from the American CIA? Is it true that Christians are against the Revolution?"

I answered, "The true Christian does not belong to the Left nor the Right."

The Cuban was unyielding, "You must be on one side or the other!"

"No," I weakly assured him, "I am only on the side of Christ. I am not fighting for things on the earth. Our kingdom is in heaven."

"That is the philosophy the gringos have given you. Such things don't exist. You must be on our side. If you aren't, some of you are going to die. We have killed a lot of people such as you who decided not to be on our side."

Again, a Security Agent would push my head under the water while the black Cuban gave the orders. One minute under and one minute out I would go. While under, I was hit. I thought I was going to die. There were pains all over my body.

Those doing this torture knew exactly how long I could take this "treatment." The Vulture and the Furious One took part in this torment.

Then I was moved to a large cell with a very bad odor: feces on the floor and different types of insects, including cockroaches, mosquitoes, and fleas. I was forced to sleep on the floor for two nights while listening to screams and cries of prisoners being tortured. This really got to me.

After coming into my cell with another exchange of words, the Cuban began kicking me with his boots and hitting with his fists upon all portions of my body. Because of the lack of food and with this abuse, I fell to the floor.

Shouting, he asked me what sort of a person I was that could die for a "false philosophy" and not for "our cause," as he put it.

Physically and mentally exhausted, I was not able to control myself and began to weep. With pain running throughout my whole body, I replied, "You are in the wrong. I know Christ lives. I feel him within my heart."

He came back with, "You'll dry up in prison like a piece of dried fruit."

When the captors left my cell, I continued weeping as I thought about my family when a light appeared. Distinctly, I heard a voice speaking to me, "My servant, remember that some days ago, I spoke to you and said that you would take the church to another place. I am the same one who took Peter out of prison; preserved Shadrach, Meshach, and Abednego from the fiery furnace; kept Daniel from the lions; and led my people out of Egypt. I will take you out because stronger is the one with you than the one ruling in the world. You must trust me. I tell you, only be strong. Don't be afraid because I will be with you."

After hearing this, I began to cry again. But this time, I was praising the Lord, as I knew he was going to take me out of this situation.

Now, the "Cobra" entered my experience in prison. Stepping into my cell, he informed me that I was to be placed before a firing squad. Taking me to a small courtyard where there were both men and women soldiers, he ordered me to take off my clothes. As I did this, Cobra called out to the soldiers, "Look at the 'Little Pastor.' His God never came to save him. Now he is going to feel our justice."

The soldiers laughed.

Told to dress, I was taken to another prison section, not too far away, where I was placed in front of a firing squad containing about fifteen soldiers. Standing about thirty feet from them, I heard the command, "Fire!" accompanied only by the clicking guns, with no bullets coming out. Two more times this was done.

In the cell, I was given an injection. I think because of this, even today, I tend to forget things. When memorizing Bible verses, I am not able to recall as I was accustomed.

"People Must Know"

I don't remember many things concerning my suffering. I think that I may have consciously decided not to remember what the Sandinistas did to me. But as God told me to tell others what was done by these people, I feel that God is helping me remember.

Five more days passed before I was taken, at about three in the afternoon, to a State Security Office within the prison. An official told me that a pastor had come and had put in a good word for me. He said, "We are going to allow you to go home. I want you to know that in all of the time you've been in prison, you have been here because we wanted you to experience and enjoy an 'ideological diversion.' Don't think of going to another country and tell what happened to you here. If you do this, your situation will become very bad."

The officer stressed that the La Paz-Murra Church and myself must go to the Sandinista-organized meetings and that I must not state to anyone that Christ is alive and is coming again. If I wanted to preach in places away from the congregation, I had to secure the state's permission.

I was taken from the prison and dropped off at a public park in Esteli. My hair was long, dirty, and filled with lice. My watch, billfold, belt, shoes, socks, and Bible had not been returned. Walking to an Evangelical church, I was given money from its brethren to return to La Paz-Murra.

Every four days, I had to make an appearance at the State Security Office in Murra to report what I was doing.

On the evening of September 7, I and seventy-five souls, men, women and children, began walking to get out of Nicaragua. We walked six days and six nights. Most of the time, we were without food. On one occasion, God brought us to some guayaba fruit,[1] which we ate with thanksgiving.

On the seventh day, our group crossed the Nicaraguan-Honduran border at the Poteca River where the Oro Brook enters from Honduras. We continued walking to El Oro-Trojes. There we were received very well by Honduran officials, who for two days took care of our food and lodging in a public school.

Within a day we walked to La Fortuna and stayed one day. From there the Honduran Red Cross transferred us to the refugee camp at Jacaleapa for six days and then to the other refugee camp at Teupasenti where the congregation remained to the present time.

Instead of the original seventy-five members that entered Honduras, the congregation now has eight hundred.

Fifteen days after the La Paz-Murra members left their home base, my wife and children and her parents were escorted to Honduras by the Contras. Because I was at a refugee camp and not able to leave without permission, I was not able to visit my family for six months.

Since then, I've served congregations in and near Teupasenti and at present I am residing in Tegucigalpa.

Though reminded of the Sandinista threat, I am much more concerned that people in the United States, Canada, and in Central America know the truth about Communists.[2] Their philosophies and theories are not from God. They are satanic. These Communists warned me of their retaliation, but I know that God will continue to be beside me. So will He be with all who place their trust in Him.

Diego Lacayo Oyanguren

Tegucigalpa, Honduras

August 10, 1987

> Though family heritage, history and prosperity were good
> for a sense of well-being and stability, survival was more
> important.

Leaders in Nicaragua

VERN: How long has your family been in Nicaragua?

DIEGO: In 1736 the first Lacayo, Jose Antonio Lacayo de Briones, came as a governor to Costa Rica from Spain. Later, because of civil unrest in Leon, Nicaragua, he settled and died there.

Today, the Lacayo family is one of the largest in Nicaragua with other branches in Honduras, Guatemala, and a few in Costa Rica.[1]

My mother's last name, Oyanguren, originated from the Basque region of Spain when my mother's father's father came to Nicaragua about 1915.

One of my mother's grandfather's brothers, Benito Oyanguren, became a well-known Jesuit priest in Leon where he was very much beloved. He died there about thirty years ago.

Sometime after my mother's grandfather arrived, he married my great-great-grandmother, who was from the Cardenal family, a well-known Nicaraguan name but very much split by the present political situation.

To highlight names from this family will give a good glimpse as to what has happened. Two Cardenal brothers are within the present Cabinet of the Sandinista government: Ernesto,[2] a writer and poet, is the Minister of Culture and Sports while Fernando is the Minister of Education.

Ernesto is getting tired of his government post. He wants to return to Solentiname, a group of islands near the Costa Rican border. There he once had established an international artists colony which was later destroyed by Somoza when the colony's political direction became evident.

He is no longer functioning as a priest after being forbidden by the Pope to do so along with his brother, Fernando.

On the other side of this family, there is a Cardenal who is the widow of Jorge Salazar, the prominent coffee grower and honorable Nicaraguan leader who was murdered by the Sandinistas. She served on the board of the Freedom Fighter group, the FDN.[3]

The editor of *La Prensa,* Pedro Joaquin Chamorro Cardenal, was killed in 1978. He was a first cousin to my mother.

Both sides of my family were always opposed to the Somoza family, but my father, though a lawyer, never got involved in politics.

My father's oldest brother built most of the roads in Nicaragua and served as the Minister of Construction for about twelve years before the last Somoza. Later, after getting into trouble with a Somoza, he left Nicaragua and worked with the World Bank for the rest of his life.

Another brother had one of the biggest construction firms in Nicaragua, the Cardenal Lacayo Fiallos.

VERN: What year were you born?

DIEGO: 1955. I am the fifth in the family of four sons and three daughters. My oldest brother, Antonio, married Pedro Joaquin Chamorro's daughter. He considered becoming a Jesuit priest and went through five years of that society's higher education, but he decided against it and went to various educational centers in the United States. He received a degree in Industrial Engineering from the Institute of Technology in Georgia. He then earned a Master's in Industrial Engineering at MIT and a Master's in Finance at Harvard.

A married sister lives in Chicago; a married brother works for a multinational company in Mexico; and a married brother, a married sister, and a single sister live in Miami.

There, the married sister's husband is Alfredo Sasa, a very young and sharp individual, who is one of the Nicaraguan Resistance leaders.

VERN: All are outside Nicaragua?

DIEGO: All except Antonio. Not one to involve himself in politics, though his wife is one of the owners of *La Prensa,* which has been closed for a year now, he does not want to leave Nicaragua. He is a partner of a business group owned by a Boston banker, a very wealthy family in San Salvador, and Adolfo Robelo, a Freedom Fighter leader. This group has investments in Nicaragua, big ones such as factories and industries; investments in Costa Rica, with one partner, that country's president, Oscar Arias, involving sugar and coffee; and in Mexico where there are interests in vegetable oil and poultry.

Antonio travels a lot, even in the United States. He feels that some day everything will change in Nicaragua and thus the money of Nicaragua, the cordobas, that come from company profits are invested in the purchasing of farm buildings, lands, and other properties. It may be that this group will be the largest of its kind in Central America.

The government hasn't really messed with my family. In '82 the government did confiscate one of my father's businesses, sugar distribution which he conducted on a national basis, but it hasn't touched anything else. My father still has the trucking business which transports sugar and coffee to the ports. This business, however, is almost dead. There are no parts available in Nicaragua for Mack trucks.

My folks travel a lot visiting their children, to my home, Mexico, Chicago, and to their home in Miami. My mother has a Spanish passport, which helps. At sixty-eight, my father prefers the environment which he is used to, though Nicaragua may be hard pressed with troubles.

"A Place of Danger"

VERN: Would you tell a little about your education?

DIEGO: Jesuits conducted my elementary education. They were part of our family tradition; my mother's brother is also a priest.

All went well until 1967 when I began to have difficulties in comprehending the Jesuit educational stress. A new generation of Jesuits had come within a Marxist framework, and it became wrong to attend our parties and celebrations. It was not proper to dress nicely. We had to go to help poor people. There were lots of emphases such as this.

VERN: What sort of a school was this and what happened?

DIEGO: This institution was a high school, a Jesuit school for the wealthy. We had about a thousand students enrolled. Formerly in Granada, it was now located in Managua and called Colegio Centro America.

VERN: Were all of the teachers at the school sympathetic to the Left?

DIEGO: No, no, there were three or four.

As it all turned out, I thank God that I got into a problem at the Jesuit school and was forced to enroll at the Christian Brothers school, La Salle,[1] which belongs to an international system throughout the world. The Brothers were different and didn't deal with students as the Jesuits had. They prepared me academically, physically, and spiritually. They were not Marxist in viewpoint. They were not with the emphasis of the Popular Church and were not a part of the movement promoting Liberation Theology and the ideology of the Left.

In November 1972, in my seventeenth year, I graduated from La Salle. I had plans to study in the States, but this was canceled because of family financial losses due to the earthquake in December. As my father was already handling the education of four children abroad, he allowed me to go to San Salvador where I attended the Jesuit University.[2]

There, I sensed that everything was just beginning in the manner of the Left that I had experienced earlier in Managua. Though I knew a number of men from Nicaragua who were becoming priests and knew what they were thinking, they didn't mess with me.

Concluding one year in El Salvador, I went to the University of Georgia at Athens, the home of the Bulldogs, and in December 1976 received a B.A. degree in Business Administration.

As 1977 was the best economic year Nicaragua had ever had, a boom year, and with my estimation that financial opportunities were very good, I wanted to be employed with my father. Instead, I joined Eastern States Standard Oil, now called EXON because of antitrust laws. ESSO was a very,

very good school for me and probably the biggest company in Nicaragua, not on the employee side but in the volume of money. Five or six times a year, I was encouraged to study outside the country.

In January of 1978 at the time of the murder of Pedro Joaquin Chamorro, big trouble began brewing in Nicaragua and everybody turned against Somoza.

VERN: Would you say that Somoza was neither a dictator nor a good democrat?

DIEGO: Somoza wasn't bad, not even half as bad as the present guys are. Though he did develop the country, his father was an even better man who worried about the nation's development in such areas as cattle and cotton growing. He gave lots of money to the National Bank who in turn lent it to those who had the capacity to develop the country.

The last Somoza was degenerate and surrounded himself with very bad, very stupid people. Following the earthquake he gave the Left the opportunity they had been hoping for. The worldwide assistance, canned food, tents, and all sorts of supplies, millions of dollars worth that poured into Nicaragua, were stolen by corrupt army men who aided in weakening the nation.

The Sandinistas were beginning to be noticed. As a result, their access to the people was made easier because everyone was angry at Somoza.

To further complicate the mess he was getting into, Somoza threw out his wife and appeared with a mistress, Dinorah.[4]

As times became more corrupt, Somoza began to compete with the wealthy, and together with other things provoked a rebellion against himself.[5]

VERN: I have heard that the campesinos didn't care one way or another. It was the middle class and wealthy that realized that they weren't being given their fair share.[6]

DIEGO: Right. In towns such as Esteli in the northern part of Nicaragua, Sandinistas would attack the community with ten or fifteen men and began shooting at the command post. Individuals within the town then would aid the Sandinistas by building street barricades and opening holes in the walls of houses.

Following the battle the invaders would leave and hide in the mountains, but people within the city would be forced to face the irritation of the military forces during the cleanup operation. Any young person with a wound on the arm or knee would be suspect and stood a chance of being shot. Merely an accusation could bring death. Many young men were killed in this manner, and their relatives began to take the side of the Sandinistas.

In reality, it was the Sandanistas who provoked the situation. They knew exactly what they were doing.

When the Sandinistas went to another city to execute the same tactic, everyone knew what the military would do when they came in force. Though thousands fled without guns, the Sandinistas had what they needed, poor people from the towns to do their bidding when arms came.[7]

Before the Sandinista takeover, there were two general strikes in Nicaragua. Though our General Manager didn't want us to, stressing that the company was nonpolitical, we employees of ESSO went on strike.

With the overthrow completed, all of us regretted what we had done. How stupid we were to have helped these new guys out!

In 1980, I got married and in 1982 was sent by ESSO to Coral Gables, Florida, for a two-year study concerning an oil-blending process to be used in Corinto, Nicaragua, and another plant in Panama. About eight months into the training, I was recalled to Nicaragua, as the country was losing many engineers and other talented people.

With my return in 1983 I could plainly see that things were different and beginning to change for the worse. The money exchange rate had gone from twenty-five *cordobas* to about one hundred per dollar. Whereas I had been paid in dollars, I was now given *cordobas* that were losing their value. There were no incentives given to employees. The economy was being ruined.[8]

I began to take short trips into Honduras. For a few days at a time, I began setting up a company to import and export raw materials for animal feed. Once I secured the contracts supplying these raw materials, I moved to Honduras with my family.

The Nicaraguan Minister of Finance was sorry that I was leaving and said it was too bad as I would have been a help for the Revolution and other "bullshit."

I felt like a stranger in my own country. People would look at me in a bad light. In the Immigration Office to obtain a visa, many stupid questions were asked, and I was intimidated and labeled "bourgeois." Some of those calling me such names weren't the same type of people they once had been.

I realized that one of these days one of former Sandinista friends might say that I was a Contra, a CIA contact, or some such thing.

My sense of safety was beginning to leave me, and in 1984 I left the place which was not my country anymore.

I appreciate what the Hondurans have done for me and my family. We've been given the opportunity to do business, and my import-export company has done well.

Even though there aren't many dollars in Central America, countries use trading techniques that make it possible for commerce to succeed.

When I arrived in Honduras, many suggested that I go into the Contra movement, just like the Sandinistas tried to recruit me. But I tell the Contras that I am not inclined to do such a thing because I don't like getting involved in politics.

Book II
Citizens of Eastern Nicaragua

Joraila Wallace

Tegucigalpa, Honduras

February 24, 1987

> This lady recognizes the Miskito Indian need for compe-
> tent leadership and hoped for understanding and friend-
> ship from responsible people.

"Proud Community...Subjected"

Why did Joraila desire to learn German? Though born in 1944 in the Miskito Indian[1] village of Krukira, one-fourth of her immediate family ancestry is German. Thus she wants to add German to the languages (Miskito, Spanish, and English) that she already speaks fluently.

After marrying a U.S. citizen in 1967, Joraila left with him to the States and became an American citizen in 1974.

Returning to Nicaragua's East Coast in 1978, the couple opened a rehabilitation center and special education school in Puerto Cabezas. They focused their efforts in aiding children born without limbs, described in medical terms as phocomelia.[2]

The institution reached out to the deaf, mute, blind, mentally retarded, those afflicted with cerebral palsy, etc., individuals from all over the Nicaraguan Mosquitia.

Their organization, the Nicaraguan Children's Fund, was sustained by individuals from the United States and Europe. Relatives of Joraila were important in the initial work, the only one of its kind in Nicaragua.

When the new government closed the institution in 1979, the numbers of those assisted had grown to thirty-five. Joraila and her husband, Tommy Wallace, were proud of their work.

The Wallaces sensed the new leadership's anti-American sentiment. Tommy and their seven-year-old son, Mark, fled Nicaragua just a few days before the Sandinistas took over Puerto Cabezas. Joraila remained behind to ascertain if these new political forces would sanction their work.

A different fate awaited a family friend. Santiago Miller, an American, belonged to the De La Salle Christian Brothers and served as the school principal of the Instituto Bartolome in Puerto Cabezas. After the new government takeover, Santiago went to Guatemala. There in February 1981 while he was repairing a window on an Indian church, four hooded men appeared and shot him to death.[3]

After the first few days, when anyone with the slightest connection to the former government was jailed, Sandinista leaders played along with the townspeople when the citizens demanded that all prisoners be set free.

Why did the new leaders[4] condone such a thing? Citizens had heard and believed Sandinista propaganda about "people-power." They were allowed to witness the gathering of most of the town's prisoners in the local park. As each detained individual was presented to the crowd, it voted as to who would be released.

The few still in custody included former National Guard officers. Though it was stated at the time that they also would be freed, instead, Sandinista authorities began killing them.

As almost every one of the detainees was guiltless, close relatives began pestering the local dignitaries to set them free. Instead, the Sandinistas began the process of exchanging captives from other sections of the nation.

Joraila explained what type of person the new government selected to lead the denizens of the Puerto Cabezas area. He was a young man who appeared to be a college student, a young punk. She lamented that the proud community of Puerto Cabezas had been subjected to such a turn of events.

Next came the organizing of the Community Block Committee or CDS, whereby within each city section a person was placed in charge of registering everyone.

Because government propaganda emphasized how the prosperous should be sharing with those who were not well-off, the poor went along. Many among the poorer class of people assented to Sandinista actions when Chinese merchants[5] were being picked on and charged with overpricing staples such as rice, flour, etc.

The officials smoothly introduced rationing.

When locals were asked to attend government meetings on Sundays, those refusing could be kept from receiving rationed food.

Though her institution had been politically neutral, the new authorities accused Joraila of being a Somocista. Eventually, Joraila was placed under house arrest and guards were posted at the institution.

Feeling that she was being treated very unfairly, Joraila left the property when the desire came, to go to the movies, etc. But she was always very careful to make sure that she returned. Thus validating her credibility among the Sandinistas, Joraila was able to build confidence among those who day and night guarded her.

She decided that a method of escape had to be developed. The Sandinistas did not know that she was an American citizen and carried that nation's passport.

The time arrived for Joraila to execute her escape plan. An ambulance stopped at the front of the closed institute one day when there was no guard around. Joraila got into the vehicle, lay on the floor, and covered herself with a rug. The driver had come to Puerto Cabezas to fetch supplies and was returning to the Coco River region.

Met by a guide at the Coco who took charge of her exodus, she was escorted across the river in a boat. Walking through long jungle stretches, fording another large river by canoe, and riding horseback through vast stands of pine trees, finally toward evening on the third day, Joraila came to a Miskito village.

Why did Joraila make such a laborious journey after crossing into Honduras on the first day? At the time, the vast Honduran Mosquitia served the Sandinistas like a free zone between countries. It was best to travel far into Honduran territory to avoid Sandinista patrols.

The next day, Joraila was relieved to learn that a small plane might be setting down upon the local landing strip to pick up a few teachers.

A plane belonging to Alas de Socoro (Wings of Help) of Missionary Aviation Fellowship did land. It took off with Joraila aboard and winged its way to Puerto Lempira.

She was given permission the following day to fly in a Honduran military aircraft to Tegucigalpa. Then it was on to Guatemala, Houston, and San Antonio, Texas.

No One to Relate Stories to

By now, the government had seized the Wallaces' farm and another parcel of land, the Ford F150 pickup with an attached camper, and everything else. Though the title to the car, purchased in Texas, remains in Joraila's possession, the vehicle too had been confiscated when she was still in Puerto Cabezas.

Before her house arrest, Joraila had been invited to travel to Managua to participate in a fifteen-day cultural exhibition. She accompanied others of her people displaying Miskito art forms including song, dance, and music.

She heard Tomas Borge, who had come to the dressing room, promise Miskito Indians that the new government would conquer hunger. Then he pompously declared that the first man whom he would send to the moon would be a Miskito Indian.

Joraila has since wondered if going to the moon equals going down six feet. It has been charged that East Coast citizenry were snatched from their homes. In the middle of the night, these people were taken to isolated, moonlit locations, places of lonely torture, to be extorted for confessions and then be locked up. A hand or a foot of one of the many who were forcibly ordered to dig a hole, shot, and covered up was frequently discovered by townspeople walking along the beach.

Those jailed, all frightened and intimidated, were warned upon pain of death never to speak about their detention, torture, and questioning. This brainwashing was effective. The living conditions, including disease and lack of care within the jails, often resulted in death.

Joraila stressed what the Sandinistas afflicted upon the Miskitos was much more gigantic and horrifying than she could describe.

She told of a Miskito mother who sadly narrated how her thirteen-year-old son's death was about to take place. Captives of the Sandinistas, he and seven other captives had their hands and feet tied, with their bodies weighted down. They were about to be placed aboard an aircraft in order to be cast somewhere into the Caribbean. As the son was about to be taken aboard, one of the guards said, "Why don't we leave him?"

Another guard insisted that he be taken, but the first guard persisted and the boy was left.

Instead of drowning him, the Sandinistas blinded him with lighted cigarettes. Though his mother requested that artificial replacements be inserted, there wasn't much that Joraila could do, because funding was needed in so many other areas.

Regretting the many who have been killed and injured without anyone telling their stories, Joraila pointed fingers at American reporters who didn't seem to have the courage to tell what has been going on inside of Nicaragua. She noticed how the "left side" of the news always seemed to prevail, specifically "how nice the Sandinistas were in taking care of their people." If a negative side of the Sandinistas happened to appear in the world news, it usually ended up as the fault of the United States or just a "mistake" on the part of the new government.[1]

In the greater Waspam area alone, Joraila accounted for thirty-four communities which had been attacked by the Sandinista army. Miskito inhabitants were driven from their land and homes, leaving their societies violently disrupted.[2] Women and girls were raped, cattle killed, productive trees cut down, and many starved. Joraila charged the Sandinistas with deliberately forcing the citizenry onto unproductive lands.

Some who had been moved and detained were guarded on land which the Wallaces owned north of Puerto Cabezas.

Joraila's uncle, a Moravian pastor,[3] was detained, tortured, and ordered not to reveal what had happened to him.

A United Nations refugee camp was a place of last resort for the refugee. Joraila believeds that the United Nations Relief Organization was not on the side of the Indians. It did not supply enough food, clothing, or sufficient medical aid.

The host government stopped granting extensions with residence visas. The squeezed had only two options: To return to Nicaragua or go directly to a refugee camp. Unemployment had risen to such a high rate in Honduras that its government was forced to prevent new refugees from entering the country.

Miskito Indian Politics

During our interview, I asked Joraila about Miskito Indian politics. The Indian region of eastern Nicaragua believed Sandinista promises (democratic government, land rights, and individual freedoms) and a new representative assembly was to have been formed to replace the old one, ALPROMISO. It was to cover the same geographical sector: a large portion of the Caribbean Coast region within the Department of Zelaya.

Daniel Ortega, before he was inaugurated as president, came to the assembly meeting with Sandinista Party bureaucrats and such dignitaries as Father Obando Bravo. It was unusual for Nicaraguan officialdom to give recognition to East Coast people by its coming out into the area. With Sandinistas bestowing new titles upon the locals, the assembly was thought to be unique.

Joraila remembered Daniel Ortega telling the assembly, "I think the following name is very good." He was proposing a new title to replace ALPROMISO[1] with the words "Miskito, Sumo, Rama, Sandinista…MISURASATA." Joraila said that he stressed being united and used the words *kupia kumi*, which is Miskito for "one heart."[2]

The assembly had not been difficult to manage as the delegates were mainly elementary schoolchildren and some from high school. The very few who had college studies were among the leadership.

Steadman Fagoth Muller, a local leader, was in his early twenties. That he was being used by the Sandinistas to make it appear that the government was cooperating with the Indians was becoming very clear to Joraila. Steadman never went along with the insertion of the Sandinista name[3] within the new organizational name, MISURASATA, and he knew that the Indians were hoping to become independent. Surreptiously, he told Miskitos to keep the name, but to remember that they were not to be in one spirit with the Sandinistas. But when he threw a large party to present his plan for the Miskitos, the Sandinistas charged that he had gone too far and placed him under lock and key.

The local population now rallied around him. Miskitos told the Sandinistas that if they didn't release Steadman there would be a big war.

When Steadman was brought back to Puerto Cabezas under guard, the Sandinistas had plans to kill him. But he was given permission to visit his mother along the Coco River, and he escaped into Honduras. There, he and Joraila had a conversation via telephone.

Joraila said that the biggest problem for the Miskitos in Honduras was that they didn't have good leadership. Steadman did things which he should not have done. Eventually, he was replaced. But because the new leadership had done no better, Steadman was making a comeback.[4]

Through the determined propaganda effort of Tomas Borge, some Indians were seduced into returning to Nicaragua.[5] He and his Sandinista gang said they were willing to forgive the Indians. They would be allowed to return to their villages, and would be given money, free immunizations, positions, and much freedom.

Joraila still feels that these Communists cannot be trusted.[6] Her husband expressed these thoughts: "I was not in a position to sell my soul to them, neither my convictions, conscience, value, nor principles."

Joraila keenly senses the privation and suffering which the Sandinistas have brought to the Miskitos: "Lots of misery, starvation, death, separation of families, church divisions.... When my grandmother was sick, there was no way to visit her. When she died, there was no possibility of traveling to Nicaragua.

"I'm asking all freedom-loving people not to let us down."

Edwin Muller.

Edwin Muller

Tegucigalpa, Honduras

February 24, 1987

> The terrible brutalities committed by the Sandinista government made Edwin Muller realize that any form of association with it was fraught with danger.

Accounts of Atrocities

EDWIN: Twenty-five years ago, I was born in Waspam, a town along the Coco River in northeast Nicaragua.

VERN: What is your educational background?

EDWIN At the time of the Sandinista attack upon the Miskito people, I had finished high school and was planning to enroll at the university in the capital, but government problems against Miskitos made matriculation difficult.

VERN: When did the attack hit your area?

EDWIN: At the end of December 1981, a campaign of terror was imposed upon thirty-four communities along the Coco River, including Waspam.[1]

VERN: What was the population of Waspam?

EDWIN: Around three thousand.

VERN: You witnessed what happened?

EDWIN: Yes, before Waspam was emptied of its people, the Sandinista Army had gone into about ten other area communities. We heard reports of what was taking place: burning of homes and businesses, destruction of fruit trees, killing of cattle, and harm and death to human life. Then, we began to witness these same bad incidents within Waspam itself. Everyone attempted to leave for Puerto Cabezas, Managua, Honduras, which was just across the Coco, or just somewhere. Though merchants began closing their shops and taking what they could, many items were left behind.

A sad chapter to all this, I personally witnessed at the Waspam airport dirt landing strip. Here, just off the east end of the strip, lay a small lagoon, a hill, and an area of bush. I knew the place well.

One, two, or three times daily just before Christmas, a gruesome picture unfolded itself as a Bulgarian aircraft containing about fifty people was emptied of its human cargo: Miskitos from area communities. A large army truck was brought to the landing field and backed up toward the doorway of the plane. A terrible drama would be repeated as numerous soldiers would congregate to make sure that all was accomplished according to the new government's directions.

The army vehicle could not approach close enough for the aircraft to unload directly unto the truck platform, and it was frightful to watch as civilians were compelled to jump four and half feet to the ground.

This sorry sight was further complicated in that all passengers were tied with their hands to their backs, and all were bound by the same long rope with about a foot and a half between each person. When one was forced to leap, the next in line would have to jump at the same time, with all sorts of tumbling and falling the norm as victims injured themselves. Male and female, most were young, but there were the elderly and children as young as seven.

Mounting the truck platform was another ordeal as it must have been at least four feet from the ground with a foot-high baseboard. These tied, tormented, weeping, and screaming people, some with no shoes nor shirts, were forced to make this almost impossible climb. I don't know how they ever did it. To "aid" them, the guards beat them with fists and rifle butts and kicked them with shouted orders and curses.

VERN: As you already probably know, the Left within America refer to these particular actions as "Sandinista mistakes." How long did this continue?

EDWIN: Every day for three weeks before I was able to get away from Waspam. Most of the people were transported away from the airport to who knows where.

The first load was deposited in the bush only about sixty feet from the end of the runway. The truck that took these people remained in that location all day long. When people who lived at the airport saw it emerge, it was empty except for the driver and guards. There was no other place for that vehicle to exit from this small, confined site.

The first people we saw must have been killed with weapons that made no noise, such as knives, bayonets, and rifle butts. Some were most likely buried alive. The guards surely would have had victims dig their own graves, a technique used by the Sandinistas against the Nicaraguan National Guard. If a helicopter hovered over the spot, the victims could have been finished off by bullets. The noise of the aircraft's engine would have drowned out any gunfire.

A few days later when no one happened to be around, I and a friend sneaked to the spot where our people had been taken. Being extremely cautious, we saw many, many graves. As I had to work in another place during the day, I did not see every time an army truck took more Miskitos to their death.

VERN: How many graves did you see?

EDWIN: Plenty! I never thought in terms of numbers.

VERN: Did you dig into any of them to verify the evidence?

EDWIN: No, with many troops near, great care had to be taken.

VERN: I assume that graves would still be in that same location, if anyone would care to investigate.

EDWIN: If anyone went to this place today, one would find the remains.

Of all those transferred from plane to truck, only one was ever set free, a pregnant woman. Her hands had been untied and she was allowed to walk away down a road to the center of Waspam.

VERN: Did you recognize any of the soldiers?

EDWIN: A few of the guards were men from northeast Nicaragua. One of them, Roy Smith, a Creole from Tronquera and a former friend of mine, worked with the Sandinista Security forces. While landing from a helicopter, he was ambushed by Freedom Fighters at San Carlos which lies quite a ways west from Waspam.

Though a pilot on the damaged 'copter managed to escape, Roy was captured with some others. When the Freedom Fighters discovered what he had been doing, they executed him.

I saw men from Puerto Cabezas mistreating people. Of these, Filemon Rivera was the most cruel. A person of mixed blood, possibly Creole, Chinese and Spanish who could speak Miskito, Spanish, and some English, I heard that he was sent to Cuba to become a specialist in torture.

Another person from Puerto Cabezas who stands out in my mind was Jimmy. Can't remember his last name, but he was at least part Miskito and could speak Miskito, Spanish, and English. I heard a few days ago that he had been killed by the Freedom Fighters.

There were other State Security men who took part in these criminal actions whom I also recognized from area communities.

The Sandinista soldiers, on the other hand, were from the West Coast of Nicaragua.

VERN: Young soldiers disciplined and working at being loyal to an ideology which, really, was not interested in them as human beings.

EDWIN: This brings to mind another aspect as to what Sandinistas were like and how they treated their own soldiers.

In the beginning operations against the Miskito people, I think there might have been logistical problems in sending their own dead back to the Pacific region, as well as requests to explain why so many soldiers were being killed in the Mosquitia.

On one occasion, the Sandinistas brought dead bodies of soldiers by ground and air transport to this same airfield in Waspam. As it was around 7:00 P.M., trucks were formed in a semicircle with headlights centered upon long boxes, each some fifteen feet long, that were being stacked one on top of the other. There must have been about fifteen boxes.

Gasoline was thrown onto the stacked structure as well as on a length of ground leading to it. When the gasoline was lit, a stream of fire burned the distance to the boxes, with an explosion when the soaked wood ignited.

Though the evening was beautiful, as it usually was in Waspam, and the fire looked awesome, something which no one had ever seen before, after about twenty minutes, the smell of burning bodies reached to where I had positioned myself.

Each coffin contained about three soldiers.

VERN: How did you know that these bodies were soldiers?

EDWIN: Very early the next morning, some of us boys went to make sure that that which was burned were humans.

I had been warned not to go, but being very curious, I wanted to investigate and saw bones, remains of a head and a stomach, and other human body parts which were still burning.

The evidence that these were the remains of Sandinista soldiers also came from persons whom I knew, who had attended to wounded soldiers and had transported dead bodies. The Sandinistas actually burned soldiers who hadn't even died but were severely wounded. Only the corpses of higher grade officers were being sent back to the Pacific side to be buried.

"Sense Of Survival…Keenly Sharpened"

EDWIN: My escape from Waspam had to be accomplished covertly. As the military was checking everyone at the Waspam airport, I had to use a different name to reach Managua.

When my parents reached Managua two months later, they brought more awful news. Though my parents left for another community just before the total evacuation of Waspam, they still experienced how townsfolk were seized for jailing, torture, and relocation. All this was accompanied by burning down houses, tree destruction, animal killing, and even execution of people on the city streets.

VERN: How did your parents manage to travel to Managua?

EDWIN: To make a long story short, my father had an eye problem. As he was working for a government company, he got special permission to journey to the capital for treatment.

But I returned one moe time to Waspam.

VERN: With all of the danger, why did you return?

EDWIN: The family had personal property which had been left behind.

VERN: What did you notice?

EDWIN: None of the civilian population remained in town. The military had begun to destroy buildings and cultivated property. A certain section was being turned into a military base.

VERN: Three thousand no longer living as they had been.

EDWIN: Everyone gone, with many having been killed.

VERN: What did you notice about family property?

EDWIN: My sister's house was totally burned, but my parent's house was standing.

VERN: And then after your return from Waspam?

EDWIN: In June 1982, I visited Costa Rica. I thought of remaining but there were difficulties for Nicaraguans. As I only had a visa for a short visit, a couple of weeks, I returned to Managua.

It was difficult to find a job; companies would only hire on condition that a person first do time in the military. Because of this I worked at a number of short-term jobs.

If I had been a student, I would have been subject to military draft at any time. All students had to belong to one of two organizations: the Sandinista Youth "19th of July" or the Popular Militias (Milicias Populars). Needless to say, I avoided being a student. Killing other Nicaraguans or being killed by them was not what I wished on anyone. My sense of survival was keenly sharpened by the sights, sounds, and smells of a Sandinista government in Managua.

VERN: What was life like on the local city block?

EDWIN: I attended the CDS block meetings. There were those attempting to place me into a leadership position. Not appreciating the system, I never truthfully expressed myself, and in order not to be overly watched, I said that I had a scholarship to study in Russia, which I never had.

VERN: Were you a part of night guard duty?

EDWIN: Yes, it is forced upon citizens. I did this two or three times from seven in the evening to seven in the morning. If one didn't do this guard duty, he was called a Contra, the only charge that was leveled. When I was asked to do anything, I did it. One also had to participate in local block meetings which were conducted every night.

VERN: If parents were forced to attend these meetings, they wouldn't have time to be alone with their children.

EDWIN: They had to go, and they took the children along, even small babies.

VERN: How about home gatherings? How about church meetings and home Bible study groups? There would have been many of these in a city the size of Managua.

EDWIN: To have such a meeting, a special permit was required. If one had a small meeting without a permit, one would be questioned.

VERN: When did you leave Nicaragua?

EDWIN: September 1983. Everything was in order for my exit, passport, visa, bus ticket, and a friend traveling out with me. My mother began to weep. She said that she would not allow me to go as it was too difficult for her.

"Well, mother," I replied, "though I have everything ready and have planned to leave at six in the morning, if you want me to, I will remain here in this country. But remember, you will not have me at home. There are those who are catching young men and are sending them to fight. I don't like this at all. So, you will have to decide one of two choices: You are going to allow me to go to Honduras, be alive there, or allow me to fight against Nicaraguans."

A few minutes later permission was granted. There was no alternative. I would have opposed the leaders of the present Nicaraguan government. This feeling lay deeply within my heart. If I had remained, I don't think I would be alive today.[1]

When I traveled to Managua during the time of the uprooting and killing of Miskitos, I was accompanied by a couple of Miskito friends. Later, after becoming employed with a government company, they were snatched by army personnel, sent to fight, and were killed.

My country is beautiful, but the government is terrible for its people. I have known many others who were caught by the military and sent to fight the Contras. Two or three weeks later, some of these were back in Managua in their own boxes, killed after having received very limited military training. Seventeen coffins in a row. I went to the funeral.

EDWIN: It must have been about May 1982. There was an honor guard with guns and flags. Parents were weeping, and the Sandinistas were putting on their political show with some agreeing with them. Others just kept quiet, their thoughts to themselves.[2]

VERN: The procession went from a church to a cemetery?

EDWIN: There was no church involved.

VERN: The mourners were just marched.

EDWIN: From a plaza to a cemetery.

VERN: No priest around?

EDWIN: No priest around.

VERN: Some of the nine top commandantes were there?

EDWIN: Yes, I think there were a couple. One, a Mexican, and Bayardo Arce. Some lesser ranked officials were there, also.

> If the Left ever were to take over America, the number of executions would be something horrific.

Tegucigalpa, Honduras
March 28, 1987

"Man Tries One Plan, But God Has Another"

VERN: Would you introduce yourself?

TRUKSULU: Truksulu is my Freedom Fighter pseudonym. It comes from one of my Indian ancestors who fought against the Spaniards after the time of Columbus.

Born at Uhrey near Bilwaskarma on the East Coast of Nicaragua, I am thirty years of age.

VERN: What languages do you speak?

TRUKSULU: My mother tongue is Miskito. I also speak Spanish and English.

VERN: Would you give more background?

TRUKSULU: I spent the third through the tenth grades in Puerto Cabezas. Then I went to Siuna with a State Agricultural Scholarship where I was permitted to participate in sports. I wanted to enter farming and be independent regarding a future occupation. As it turned out, man tries one plan, but God has another.

After the 1979 Revolution, I returned to Puerto Cabezas for the continuation of my studies in a high school called the Instituto Bartolome Colon. I finished my fourth year but not the fifth as the Sandinistas had come up with the Alphabetization Program, the Literacy Campaign in Spanish and Miskito. I had also become a youth leader in the church and in MISURASATA.

VERN: What church did you belong to?

TRUKSULU: Moravian.

VERN: Were you present at the meeting when the name MISURASATA was proposed?

TRUKSULU: It was the fifth assembly of the Miskito population. From 177,000 Miskitos,[1] representatives from 250 towns and villages were gathered to select new officials to work in cooperation with the Sandinistas.[2]

VERN: Did you know that the Sandinistas were Communists?

TRUKSULU: Most didn't know that.

VERN: During the fighting in 1979, was there much action in the Mosquitia?

TRUKSULU: A few clashes at Bonanza, Rosita, and along the Coco River, but not much along the Atlantic Coast.

VERN: What were you doing at this time?

TRUKSULU: I was in Puerto Cabezas with one year of school to complete. I played baseball for an Indian team and was employed in a store to supplement my parent's income and aid in furthering my own education.

VERN: Did you begin hearing of citizens who met misfortune?

TRUKSULU: Sure! One of the first things that struck me was the Sandinistas' injustice done to one of our leaders, Lyster Athders.[3] They just seized Lyster, didn't tell him what his crime was, and executed him.

VERN: Would you explain how your eyes were opened to the hard, cold facts of what the Sandinistas were up to?

TRUKSULU: To answer this, it will take a little history. Though government officers began killing our leaders, our confidence was not shaken. In spite of the fact that I was employed, I felt that I should go out and help my people and the Sandinistas in the Alphabetization Program.

In order to do my part, I joined about eighty-five fellows from Puerto Cabezas in Bonanza for one week of training. Then we separated to go to various localities. I went to Prinzapolka where I remained for nearly six months.

VERN: What was your duty in the program?

TRUKSULU: I did supervision in Prinzapolka and its neighboring villages. It was a great experience.

Everything had to do with politics. Knowing that older folk wouldn't be able to comprehend even the vowels used in grammar, let alone to learn to read and write, I emphasized that the politics within the program was something Miskitos could never agree to.

Many teachers came into the Mosquitia with no ability to teach the Miskito language and were attempting to teach only Spanish. We thought they should have more interest in aiding our people with our own language.

VERN: You did something good for your people.

TRUKSULU: Sure, we could tell them about our future. But when we finished the Alphabetization Program, the Sandinistas had something quite a bit more radical to say.

Before this happened, Indian leaders of MISURASATA held a top-secret meeting. Some fifty men and women met to discuss how they could help the Indians and others on the Atlantic Coast.

VERN: What was the time and place?

TRUKSULU: Around the middle of February 1981 in a Moravian church in Twapi, a small village north of Puerto Cabezas.

We agreed to ask the government to set aside eighty percent of tax revenues raised on the Atlantic Coast to remain there and that the remaining twenty percent be given to Managua. By building schools, clinics and hospitals, our youth would assist Indians and all people living on the East Coast. If the Sandinistas aided us, we reasoned, we also had to help the Sandinista government in its work

We also discussed the problem of debt, some millions of dollars, left by the Somoza government.[4]

We noted that we had been promised many liberties. However, the Sandinista idea that "the poor and the rich would be equal" did not seem right. We realized that the rich had a right to exist along with the poor who had to be aided.

The leaders charged us that if they were killed by the Sandinistas, the others present should carry on with the proposals which we had discussed. On this we agreed, and after spending a time in prayer, the meeting was concluded.

VERN: Who were some of the leaders with you?

TRUKSULU: Fagoth, Brooklyn, Hazel, Bobby Holmes and others.

The meeting concluded at midnight, and I traveled by car to Puerto Cabezas and caught a few hours of sleep.

Awareness of Something

TRUKSULU: Being it was Sunday, I was intent upon going to a young people's church meeting in the afternoon. But I found out that the Indian baseball team, of which I had been a member, was involved in a special excitement in its attempt to best an army team. Many were calling for me to join the team so the Miskitos could answer to a reckless government action that had taken place some few hours before. At a party in the town park, a Miskito named Suarez had been killed by the Sandinistas[1.] Fagoth encouraged me to join the contest. "You have to play today!"

"No," I replied, "I'm going to church, because tomorrow, I'm leaving for Prinzapolka."

"We need you! We need you!" he responded. "Otherwise, we will lose the game!"

I got into my uniform, returned to the stadium, and received some satisfaction in knowing that there were many who wanted to watch me play.

In the eighth inning, I got my only hit and drove in a run. Then a teammate knocked me home, and the crowd went wild. We beat the Sandinista team, two to one!

Because the game finished around four o'clock, I had time to attend church services plus a MISURASATA-arranged dinner celebrating the baseball victory.

Late in the day, I left Puerto Cabezas to return to Prinzapolka by way of Rosita Limbaika, Alamikamban, and another village near Alamikamba. Two days later a boat carried me down the Prinzapolka River to Prinzapolka.

The following evening, February 20, was the time scheduled for the closing ceremony of the Alphabetization Program. An open invitation had been made to all students, relatives, and friends within the nine communities of the area.

Unexpectdly, just before the ceremony was to be held, radio reports stated that Indian leaders had been arrested and placed in jail in Managua after presenting the eighty/twenty-percent proposal. The Sandinistas had previously responded by saying that everything in the proposal looked fine except that a detailed autonomy outline should have been included. The Sandinistas were even going to invite Indian representation from other parts of the world to attend the ceremony at which all these good things would be presented.

Having been with them just a few days before, I felt very badly.

The ceremony was rescheduled to the following afternoon. Max Messen Samora and I decided to leave at five in the morning for Auka which was near Limbaika. We would be choosing eight students to represent their village for the concluding ceremony in Prinzapolka. Traveling upstream in a flat-bottomed boat, Max and I came upon a barge from Limbaika bound for Puerto Isabel. Its motor had broken down and it now lay anchored at a location called Samil. We recognized and greeted Elmer Prado, a MISURASATA leader, and others whom we knew on the barge.

A quarter of an hour later, we met a motorized canoe. In it were three military men, one of whom I recognized as "The Tiger" who had been stationed in Prinzapolka while the language program was in progress and who had been keeping a close watch on all that was going on.

"The Tiger," whose name was Andres, told us to stop while he and his party circled us once to inspect us closely. These three soldiers of Spanish backgrounds from the Pacific Coast area were to be among those killed in the evening.

VERN: Could "The Tiger" speak Miskito?

TRUKSULU: No.

Forty-five minutes later, we met a small river passenger craft containing possibly more than sixty fully-armed soldiers. To see this many troops within a rural area was extraordinary. There had been many army men around for security purposes when the Alphabetization Program had been administered in Spanish.[2]

These troops were moving into positions for military action against Miskito people. In a few hours an incident was about to occur at the large Moravian church in Prinzapolka.

Because we had outboard engine failure before returning to Prinzapolka, the closing ceremony was delayed to 6:00 P.M.

Some of the troops that I had seen earlier in the day were dropped off at Samil and Puerto Isabel. About thirty had come to Prinzapolka, a village with a population of about seventy families.

Elmer Prado, now also in Prinzapolka, approached me and told me the soldiers had come to arrest him.

Half-believing Elmer, I asked, "Really? What are you going to do?"

When thinking back on this conversation, I have sadness in my heart because a dear man, Warring Telet, comes to my memory. He was a serious, twenty-year old friend who in 1985 was killed in our fight to free Nicaragua of the Sandinistas. Not too long ago, I visited with his mother at a refugee camp in Honduras.

Warring said, "Why should Prado be taken across the inlet? Instead, let's see what the Sandinistas are up to. Why should they want to molest this small peaceful village?"

Though he suggested that all of us defend Elmer, I was still of the opinion that we should take Elmer across to safety. Because Warring insisted and others joined him, I relented and that's the way it was.

Provocation in Prinzapolka

At the evening ceremony there must have been four to five hundred in attendance. Max and I were selected to be the first speakers.

I recognized the many sacrifices Miskitos had taken upon themselves and expressed thanks to all who had done their part.

After Max, David Ro'driguez, the coordinator for the program representing the community of Prinzapolka, took his turn. Later, he lost a leg in the civil war and is receiving treatment in Albuquerque, New Mexico.

Santiago, who is now with KISAN,[1] was speaking when one of the Sandinista officers Max and I had seen earlier barged into our meeting. The officer and two soldiers with him were fully armed with automatic weapons.

When this army man announced that he had come to arrest Elmer Prado, the whole assembly was shocked. Never had they witnessed anything like this in the forty-seven years of Somoza family rule.[2] Though some escaped through the windows and doors of the church, many were the curious who remained. The church's pastor, Nanibal Wilson, stayed during the brief action that was about to take place.

Someone in the audience asked, "What did this man do?"

Abruptly replying, the officer said, "I don't want to hear anything out of you!"

Another from the audience repeated, "What did this man do?"

"No," the officer responded, "there'll be no excuse from anyone! Just ask Fagoth. He's been with him."

Someone else stated, "We have never seen anything like this in our lifetime. Why did you come into the church? Why didn't you wait until this man left?"

Another scolded, "You think you are quite a man because you came into this meeting with your weapons. Why didn't you leave them outside and then come in?"

The officer showed his agitation. "I only came to arrest this man."

"You know, we respect your government," came another expression. "We have just gone through a difficult period and sacrificed a lot. Why do you want to treat us this way?"

"My government does not respect your program," the officer said matter-of-factly.

VERN: "My government doesn't respect your program?"

TRUKSULU: Yes, this hurt the audience, deeply. Everyone had gone through lots of sacrifice in order to help Miskitos and assist the government because the Indians were striving for peaceful relations.

VERN: What sort of an officer was this?

TRUKSULU: He said he had fought eight years.

VERN: Do you remember his name?

TRUKSULU: Julio.[3]

VERN: A big man?

TRUKSULU: He stood about five-feet-six and weighed about 180 pounds, a very stout and powerfully built individual.

Someone called out, "If you kill someone in church, the world will react very unfavorably."

Very arrogantly, Julio said, "We respect no international organization. We are in charge."

"Don't you know that you are on Indian land? You have come into an Indian church. Somoza used to respect us."

Another one shouted, "Why do you want to take this man at night?" All knew the officer had been in Prinzapolka since noon.

"I just came to arrest him. That's all."

"We will bring this man to you tomorrow," someone said, looking for a way to lessen the danger of the moment.

Sharply, the officer hurled back "No!" and back toward the entrance angrily called, "Victor!"—another of the three from our morning canoe encounter. Victor Guien had a bad reputation for torturing, a skill he had learned in Cuba. Julio commanded, "Go, beat him up, and bring him out!" *"Vaya a traer a culatazo!"* in Spanish.

The audience was standing in astonishment, so the officer had to pass through many people on his way to Elmer. He had a long way to go to reach his destination.

When he got near his intended victim, Elmer raised his hands and shouted, "Kill me or take me!" and, apparently, moved forward to take the gun from Victor.

Then "Tiger," who was standing to the far right of Julio, fired his rifle so the bullet traveled among members of the audience and hit Elmer's elevated right hand.

As if by reflex, the unarmed people nearest the armed soldiers made a grab for the weapons.

I very clearly remember what Julio was doing. He was about to pull the trigger of his AK-47 which had been pointed directly at me for what seemed a long time. As if a miracle, someone thrust his weapon upward and it went off, emptying the whole magazine clip into the ceiling.

Julio died within seconds as men killed him on the spot.

Andres and Victor met the same end. They were executed with shells from their own guns.

I learned from this experience that when an enraged population decides to get rid of bad leadership no amount of guns can stop them. Those trained Sandinista killers had come prepared with lots of weapons. They were bent on killing as many of us as they saw fit.

Though I've seen many of my friends killed since then in battles, what I observed that evening in Prinzapolka was the greatest thing from God that I have ever seen.

VERN: What about Julio's two bodyguards?

TRUKSULU: When they saw their officer taken, they ran for their lives and escaped.

VERN: What about the soldiers that must have been outside?

TRUKSULU: With their officers taken, they fled.

VERN: Anyone else killed?

TRUKSULU: Yes, Junior, who was a helper for the Moravian church. Though his home village was Karawala, he lived in a house next to the church. When he heard the shooting, he wanted to get his children who were at the meeting. Soldiers outside the church shot him as he approached.

Two civilians were killed inside the building. One of them was Granisio, and I've forgotten the name of the other man. I believe they were shot from outside the church. One of the bodyguards lingered longer than the other and it was possible that he did this killing. In all, four civilians, three officers, and two other soldiers were killed.[4]

VERN: The two soldiers were killed outside the church?

TRUKSULU: Yes.

VERN: Men from inside the church went after them?

TRUKSULU: Yes, those inside went outside and shot them.

VERN: Who were wounded?

TRUKSULU: Besides Elmer, Santiago got shot in the foot.

Later, Elmer worked with MISURA. When things got bad, before Fagoth failed, he went to the States and is now in Miami.

Bows and Arrows

It was something new for the Indians to see such a show of force in a church, a new danger and tragedy within their land.[1]

Nearly all of us went to a house near the church owned by a Spanish person whose name was Dombaye. He did not appreciate our being there and was very frightened. Many others felt the same way; we now had weapons.

Then about twenty-five of us decided to walk north to Walpasiksa. Roughly fifteen minutes after we began, suddenly we saw many people coming toward us. Every one of us dropped to the sand. We were not a little pleased to discover that the group approaching us were a hundred men, all Miskitos, who were armed with twenty-two caliber rifles, bows and arrows, and whatever else in order to assist us in fighting the Sandinistas.

One may laugh at this meager show of strength, but because of what I had just experienced, I was not the one to make fun of it.

We walked to Walpasiksa where we left Elmer, who by now was in sad shape. He had lost lots of blood and was still bleeding.

We were carrying the body of Granisio, who had served as a youth worker in the church in Prinzapolka for the past two months. Others took him to be buried, but not in his home village. It was felt that the less to do with the Sandinistas the better.

Amid the genuine, there was a spy, Mauricio Cornejo, who left our group in Walpasiksa and returned to Prinzapolka in order to inform the Sandinistas that I had killed the three officers. It was not true, but it caused me to become a fugitive.

Not being welcomed in Wounta Bar, our group kept going. At Haulover, Sam Ignasio took us to a place of security where we remained for one week before going on to Wawa Bar.

Here, our plan was to attack Sandinistas in the village and make our way by boat to Honduras. But the Sandinistas had politicians with them who requested us to give up our arms, promising that almost all of us would be set free.

Wycliffe Diego, Terilio Cirilo, Norman Bent[2], all Miskito religious leaders, and others came to where we were hiding and negotiated. Then, all of us walked to the big Moravian church in Wawa where people were crying and very sorrowful.

The next day, accompanied by some pastors, our group went to Puerto Cabezas where all were freed except for Max, me, and three others.

The following day, I was interrogated by two Cubans in the home of Pastor Princilliano Mercado.

One of them asked, "Do you know that you will be condemned to thirty years in prison?"

"If God says so, what can I do about it? Do you believe in God?" I answered, knowing how these Cubans had been trained concerning these thoughts. From our youth, iwe Miskitos grew up believing in God and no one was going to change our minds on this.

My experience in the mountains with the armed group was a new one for me. My arms were sore with many scratches and I felt miserable. Emerging from this session very frightened, I came out crying. This was how I was seen by my sister and a friend.

The next day, I was told that I must quickly leave my home and country as the authorities still were accusing me of the killings. I decided to flee without hesitation. That very night, soldiers surrounded the house where I had been staying for the purpose of arresting me.

On March 3, 1981, I entered Honduras and visited my father in a small village near the ocean.

Vern: You eventually became associated with Freedom Fighters?

Truksulu: I fought with MISURASATA and trained Miskito fighters within Nicaragua.

After a disagreement with Fagoth, I went to Brooklyn Rivera in the south of Nicaragua on August 6, 1983.

One of the greatest fighters we had was Bruno Gabrielle. A great leader of men and a young guy with a clean mind, he had interest in the poor and in the freedom of democracy.

Bruno was killed and many men became scattered because they lacked leadership. My job was to reorganize them. Forced to rest for a year because of an injury, I am feeling pretty good now.

Vern: Would you make a statement that you would like to close with?

Truksulu: I come from an Indian background and am related to all humans of the world. My people have a right to be free.

Our people need to choose another system in order to serve our Lord Jesus Christ. We must help our people build schools, clinics, and whatever, and work with democratic countries to win back freedoms lost in our nation.

It is our hope that God will help leaders among the Freedom Fighters, and democratic nations such as America to understand the role which they should be playing. I'm not only asking for assistance for Miskito and other Indian groups but also for the Nicaraguan Spanish and Creole groups as well.

For freedom to pervade completely, we have to accept the root teachings of the Bible, take Jesus as our Savior, and believe in Him as God's only Son who came to die on Calvary. With this hope, we can love our people, be saved, and see God when Jesus comes to take us to live with Him, forever.

This is the greatest life for all human beings.

Eunice Hooker Sang

Mocoron, Gracias A Dios, Honduras

June 13, 1987

Eunice's unique talent and experience in the Nicaraguan
and Honduran Mosquitia offer a striking sketch of life.

"Prefer the Times of Somoza"

VERN: I'm pleased to be with Eunice Hooker Sang who together with her husband manages a restaurant, kiosk, and lodging place in Mocoron in eastern Honduras.

Eunice, please begin by telling something about yourself.

EUNICE: Born in Granada, Nicaragua, I was raised in Bluefields where I lived for eighteen years. The firstborn in the family, I was three years old when my mother died. During my youth, I used to take my school vacations in Puerto Cabezas where I visited my father.

VERN: What sort of business did your father have?

EUNICE: A ship broker. At present he is seventy-seven and lives in Managua.

VERN: What school did you attend in Bluefields?

EUNICE: Moravian School.

VERN: Eventually, you met your husband.

EUNICE: I married Don Charley in 1981 after having lived with him two years before marriage.

VERN: Did you have any children?

EUNICE: We had one who died but no more.

VERN: Living in Puerto Cabezas under Somoza, what sort of an experience was this?

EUNICE: When a person is living good, one is inclined to say that he's not living good. If one is living badly, one cries the same way. In a sense, I can't say that I was living badly in the days of Somoza. We used to work freely and do what we wanted.

This is all in contrast to today. Now, one can't find work and one is forced to comply with the authorities.

I prefer the times of Somoza than to be with these present *piricuacos*.[1]

My husband was unjustly placed in jail for six months and nearly killed by the *piricuacos* in their questioning and their trying to force him to say things which he knew weren't true.

VERN: Did they torture him?

EUNICE: They tortured him by demanding that he agree to what they were saying. This was very hard on Don Charley with his high blood pressure and high sugar content in his blood. He had to be confined for one month in the hospital. Even there, the authorities came to him every day to question and ramble on.

Because a doctor gave me some documentation, I was able to take Don Charle to his house which was to serve as his jail.

There was no possibility for work and we weren't making a living. I went to the Sandinistas requesting that we be given some liberties so we could do something.

My request was accepted, so we popped popcorn, sold it, and made our living.

Another problem caused by the Sandinistas had to do with Don Charley's twenty-three-year-old son. The Security forces had been forcing him to work for them in exchange for setting his father free, and they began demanding that he make accusations of various people, even Moravian and Catholic religious leaders. After a month of pressure, the person in authority gave him twenty-four hours to hand over accusations, including that of his own father.

We packed some clothes and left Puerto Cabezas at one o'clock the following morning.

We went to Kum which is east of Waspam. It was too dangerous to go through Waspam. We arrived in Kum at about 5:00 A.M. when someone took us by boat to Wangklawala, Honduras.

Eunice Hooker Sang.

It was September 25, 1981, and the Sandinistas hadn't begun doing their terrible crimes on any grand scale yet.

VERN: Had you known anyone who had been mistreated earlier?

EUNICE: The National Guard colonel who had stayed with us was taken and later killed.

VERN: His name?

EUNICE: Fonseca Talavera.

VERN: When did the Sandinistas come into Puerto Cabezas?

EUNICE: July 19, 1979.

VERN: When did the colonel come to your house?

EUNICE: He gave up the Port[2] at seven in the morning and came over to our house. We gave him lodging for a time before the Sandinistas took him away and that was the end of him.[3] His wife was living in Matagalpa, where her family was into big farming.

To save his life, I tried to get him to go to Honduras, but he refused. He stated that he had been good for the community. He had gone a little crazy from all that went on. Something was wrong in his head. He didn't want to go.

VERN: How old was he?

EUNICE: The same age as my husband, who is now sixty-six.

VERN: At the time of his death, he would have been around fifty-eight.

EUNICE: His daughter even married a *piricuaco*. That's the way things work out at times.

VERN: How do you answer when people say that the National Guard was crooked?

EUNICE: A police force has to do things to keep order. One can't say that the National Guard was extra tough and killed in careless ways, no.[4]

When the Sandinistas began to come in during Somoza's time, there were young people that joined them. These began to commit crimes of all sorts, theft, rape, etc., but the National Guard was blamed.[5]

Don Charley used to tell me about the Sandinistas coming up, and I used to observe the young students at the university in Managua. They'd talk about the faults of leadership, including the living styles of people in Managua. These students were even speaking out against their own mamas and papas.

I used to ask my papa, "Hey, Pop! Why are the young getting involved with drugs? Why are they bossing everybody on everything?"

My dad was a Conservative and a good friend of Pedro Chamorro. They knew each other from their youth, and they used to study together. My dad helped Chamorro a lot.

Somoza came from the Liberal Party and didn't like my dad at all. Every time something happened in Nicaragua, the government would place my dad in jail, house arrest. So went the politics between Conservatives and Liberals.

VERN: What was his name?

EUNICE: Ernesto Hooker.

VERN: A very English name. Your husband appears to have a Chinese name.

EUNICE: Both his parents were Chinese.

VERN: There were a number of people with oriental backgrounds living in Puerto Cabezas?

EUNICE: Plenty.

"He Is a 'Jifilifi'!"

VERN: What sort of business did you and Charley have in Nicaragua?

EUNICE: Bus transportation, two passenger buses between Puerto Cabezas and Waspam.

Leaving the Port at seven in the morning, I used to reach Waspam at twelve noon and return to Port at four or five. Both Charley and I used to collect tickets.

Two more buses serviced the mining areas west of Puerto Cabezas. One made a run from Waspam and Puerto Cabezas and the other from Puerto Cabezas. Our buses held fifty passengers.

VERN: Is it true that by being accused of being a Somocista one's property would be confiscated?

EUNICE: Yeah, they wouldn't take a poor person's house. For the Sandinistas as everyone was a Somocista, they took the best they could get their hands on.

VERN: Who moved into these houses?

EUNICE: Sandinista police and leaders. Cubans came in to take over the hospital and schools. The Moravian and Catholic schools were taken over.

VERN: Where did the home owners go?

EUNICE: Ran away. Jureidin, the owner of a number of shrimp and lobster boats in Port, had the best house, worth two hundred thousand dollars. His was the first taken. Lots of nice houses were taken including that of Mr. Guthrie.[1]

VERN: What was his occupation?

EUNICE: He used to work with my dad. Also a ship broker, he had the next nicest house in town.

VERN: Who got his?

EUNICE: Those same *piricuacos*.

VERN: The Sandinistas wanted to take over your business?

EUNICE: They wanted to take over our buses, but we destroyed them. Don Charley's daughter threw sugar into the gas tanks.

VERN: Where is she now?

EUNICE: In the States. When we came to Honduras, the Sandinistas locked her up.

VERN: Was she married?

EUNICE: No. She was a young girl of twenty-three.

VERN: How long did they keep her in jail?

EUNICE: Two weeks.

VERN: Was she tortured?

EUNICE: No. She played sick and told them that she needed to see a doctor. Through friends she was given permission to see a doctor, and this was the road for her to get out of Nicaragua.

VERN: What is her name?

EUNICE: Selita.

VERN: Were there many who came to Puerto Cabezas from other parts of the world to aid the Sandinistas?

EUNICE: We called them all *piricuacos*.

VERN: The Sandinistas were accusing you working people of being rich.

EUNICE: Bourgeois and *Jifilifi*, pronounced "Hee-fee-lee-fee" in Spanish.

VERN: "High liver?"

EUNICE: Yeah. We, the "high livers," were hard workers. It became more complicated when Charley got sick and wasn't able to work. The day he was thrown in jail, I had just gotten back from Waspam. After that, I no longer worked on the bus. A boy took my place.

Charley and I were friends of the police and the National Guard including its colonels. This was a natural thing as we were in business and in the public eye. My husband had American friends and belonged to the American Club twenty-five to thirty years ago. The club had a connection with the United Fruit Company. When the club building burned down, that was the end of Charley's connection.

When the Sandinistas accused Charley of being with Americans, the accusation was based upon this association from many years before.

Charley was a member of the Lions Club for twenty years. Though this group had helped many Nicaraguans in their education or whatever, the Sandinistas didn't like this organization either.

When Charley was in jail, I used to carry his ice water in a thermos. I also brought him a mattress and a hammock. The jailer's reaction was, "Why are you bringing all of this?" Then he added, "He is a 'Jifilifi'!"

"Stupid Ones! They Are Going To Kill You!"

VERN: You were at the jail when there was some civility. Things got worse?
EUNICE: Yeah, a lot more killings. These still are going on. Even some of those who fell for Sandinista propaganda have been killed.

Sandinistas change everything. They want one to change the way one eats, sleeps, dresses, and other things. When they saw me wearing my jewelry, they said, "Why do you wear this?"

I replied, "Because I work for it." I had lots of jewelry.[1]

"Why do you have those clothes on?" they persisted. "Why don't you buy things that are more important?"

"I work for what I want," was my answer. "You can't tell me what I must buy. I eat what I want and do what I want."

"No," they said, "all of this has to change. You've got to get a uniform."

Later, I had to sell my jewelry. Charley and I weren't working and we had to eat. The Sandinistas didn't get the jewelry, but they did get the household goods when we fled.

Officials wanted us to go to meetings to hear what they wanted us to hear and to begin the process of spying on other businesses.

It wasn't my duty to snoop into other people's business, to spy on my neighbor next door. Charley and I went to no such meetings that encouraged this sort of thing. But not going did cause problems for us.

VERN: Were you called any names?

EUNICE: No. Because I was Mr. Ernesto's daughter, officials didn't notice me so much, as Mr. Ernesto was a big man, then. When I left for Honduras, not much was said about me.

I got the surprise of my life when I saw how my father had changed. I used to open my eyes wide with wonder and say to Charley, "Why can't they be as they were? Everyone is changing under the new pressure!"

VERN: When did the Sandinistas begin to place people in prison?

EUNICE: After we left. The disappearances started in October, November, and December 1981.

VERN: You had friends who just vanished?

EUNICE: Yeah, if they disappeared, one only can say that they had been killed. Those who couldn't get away were arrested.

On July 19 in Waspam, while doing my usual bus work, I talked to two soldiers with the National Guard. I said to them, "Hey! Get out of here! They've entered the Port, and they are going to kill you. Go! Run!"

"We haven't received any orders yet," was the reply. "We can't leave."

Not wasting any punches, I said to them, "You two stupid ones! Go on! They are going to kill you!"

The reply came back, "We can't do it."

One was a Miskito and the other was Spanish. The Miskito ran away and saved his life, but the other was caught and killed. Sandinistas killed all whom they knew to be soldiers. In the east area of Nicaragua, it was too much of a problem to place them in prison. The officer that came to us was tortured, killed, and buried in the sand at Twapi, north of the Port.

VERN: Just before fleeing, you and Charley were still living in your house.

EUNICE: Yes, when Charley's daughter fled to Honduras, it was then that the Sandinistas took it.

VERN: Who got your house?

EUNICE: The Bishop bought it.

VERN: The Bishop?

EUNICE: Monsignor Schlaefer.

VERN: Oh yes, he was the Catholic Bishop who led that whole village of about a thousand Miskito Indians from Francia Sirpe. The Bishop just happened to be in the village at the time and acted as a true shepherd.[2]

EUNICE: He himself was in ill health.

Because our house stood across from the Catholic church, Monsignor Schlaefer didn't want any problem that might arise with someone else that might own the property.

"So Keep Your Mouth Shut!"

VERN: When did you first began your business in Honduras?

EUNICE: We came to Puerto Lempira without any money. Because God was with us, we had friends who gave us credit to open a restaurant.

Hondurans didn't appreciate our being there. They claimed that we came to take away their food and this and that. We fought with them for two years.

I had cooks from Nicaragua. One boy used to cook Chinese foods in Managua. By preparing more types, American, Spanish and others, we had army people eating with us. The other restaurant people could do nothing about it.

But there came a time when a restaurant was needed here in Mocoron and my husband asked me to come. It was the World Relief organization that was in back of this. After three more months in Puerto Lempira, I left to be with him.

VERN: Let's see, you came to Mocoron in 1984?

EUNICE: Three years in August. Before the refugees came, there were four or five Honduran houses in Mocoron. Because of the refugees, World Relief began building roads, lights were installed, and a preparation was made for receiving more people into the community.

Today, there are about one hundred Honduran families out of a total population of three thousand people. If one has a residential visa, one can work or begin a business. In this matter, World Relief has helped some get started.

VERN: Is it true that many refugees weren't interested in coming into a town?

EUNICE: Yes, but when the Hondurans[1] saw this, they didn't appreciate it and complained that Nicaraguans had come to take over their land.

They do not want the refugees to go to the river to catch fish and iguanas nor cut any wood. The Nicaraguans musn't touch anything. They don't want refugees to sell wood as they think refugees are finishing off their pines. If the pines burn, the Hondurans blame us.[2]

When these Hondurans complain, I tell them, "You are all living good because of the refugees. So keep your mouth shut! Because of the refugees, you have lights, water, roads, good houses, and other things."

VERN: Simply and clearly stated.

I have observed people visiting this weekend from another part of Honduras who have come for a convention of the Church of God. This group was singing this morning at five.

EUNICE: They continue all night when they worship.

VERN: I noticed the Moravian church whose structure is easily identifiable as one enters Mocoron.

EUNICE: It is where the Honduran Moravians worship. Moravian refugees have their own place of worship.

The Catholics, actually, have three places for worship, Honduran and two others for Nicaraguans. Father Hugo[3] serves all of them and comes out on the last Sunday of each month. He first conducts services for the soldiers at the Honduran Fifth Battalion Headquarters a few miles south of Mocoron and then comes over here.

VERN: How about the other Sundays in Mocoron?

EUNICE: A specially designated layman offers services on the other Sundays.

Another church recently came to Mocoron, the Assembly of God.

As far as medical aid is concerned, Moravians have tried to do some things. Catholic nuns[4] from Puerto Lempira bring in medicines. They come to the church, distribute them, and check on those who are sick. Back in Puerto Lempira, they sell good medicines at a reasonable price.

Carlos Muller Schrader.

Carlos Muller Schrader
Mocoron, Gracias A Dios, Honduras
June 14, 1987

> Carlos, a Miskito and former Freedom Fighter, lauds the difficult resistance work against the Communist government of Nicaragua.

"They Cleaned Everybody Out"

CARLOS: My name, Carlos Muller Schrader, has Germanic background with the Schrader name coming from my mother and the Muller from my father.

VERN: I am surprised at the number of Miskito I have met who are connected with the Muller name.

CARLOS: The name came into Central America in 1925 through a father and son who married sisters.

VERN: Where were you born?

CARLOS: Bilwaskarma in 1939. Located on the Coco River about a six hours walk from Auka, Honduras, it's more or less twelve miles east from Waspam. It was one of the villages where everyone was cleared out by the Sandinistas. No one was left. They cleaned everybody out, all the way to Raiti, and no villages were left.

I lived in Puerto Cabezas.

VERN: I heard that the officer in charge turned the city over to the Sandinistas who then killed him.

CARLOS: That was Julio Fonseca. Don't remember his last name. It looks as if he touched up with those who came in. But they put him in jail, tortured him, and cut him up, allowing flies to infect his wounds so that worms caused him to die.

How do I know this? A fellow prisoner acted as if he were crazy and was let go. He let people know how Fonseca died.

When the Sandinistas took over, they killed lots of people. There are places where one can find bones, a pile of them.

VERN: Did you have friends who were killed?

CARLOS: Yes, one died with his father, mother, and two brothers. His name was Larry. He and his family were from Karata, south of Puerto Cabezas. The government said he was a Contra.

Nights in Nicaragua, one cannot sleep well. If I don't like you, it's easy to go and tell the authorities that you help Contras.

VERN: How old were you when you moved to Puerto Cabezas?

CARLOS: Twelve. After I finished the sixth grade, I began to work. In these days, only those who had money could go further in studies. I got a job with a company and was fortunate to study a correspondence course from California in the field of mechanics. This is what I've been working at for about ten or eleven years, buy old junk cars, fix them over, and sell them. It's how I make my living and it has been all right.

VERN: What made you leave Puerto Cabezas?

CARLOS: If the Sandinistas had caught me, they would have killed me. The day I left, they surrounded my house. They said that I helped the Contras. They'd been after me before but couldn't catch me.

VERN: Were you working with the Contras?

CARLOS: If they needed help for charging a battery or some such thing, I did it. Mostly, I worked with women right under the noses of them *piricuacos*.

VERN: How did you make your way to Honduras?

CARLOS: I took a plane to Managua and from there to Matagalpa. I got in with the Contras. They fight a battle of revenge and do it bravely.

VERN: How long did it take to make your contact with the FDN?

CARLOS: Four or five days after I got to Matagalpa. This was in 1984.

VERN: How long did you remain with them?

CARLOS: Ninety-eight days.

VERN: You told them that you wanted to go into the area in Honduras where the Miskito refugees were?

CARLOS: No problem. They help any person. Though they don't trust you at first, but this passes. After three or four days, they treat a person well. The Contras help lots of civilians and protect them. I was under Commandante Tonio when I was with them.

Great care had to be taken as the Sandinista helicopters are very dangerous. Only missiles could shoot them down. One could observe the pilot watching us and laughing, but we couldn't touch him with sixty-millimeter shells. If we could have hit the helicopter's tail rotor, we would have shot it down. We didn't have opportunity as it would quickly turn and open up with what sounded like seventeen machine guns at one time. When we heard the sound of such an aircraft, everyone would hide. These Soviet MI-24s were very swift and dangerous.

VERN: When you left the Contras, how did you reach the East Coast area of Honduras?

CARLOS: I came into Honduras at Las Vegas and from there to Tegucigalpa. The FDN sent me to the MISURA office, and then I came to Mocoron.

From the beginning I've had big sons fighting with the Freedom Fighters. They used to go to Nicaragua with a knife and a small rope to choke the *piricuacos*. This is how they got arms, clothes, and equipment. No one aided them. Our boys went by night, and I never knew for months if they were alive or not. They made them *piricuacos* jump. However, plenty of our men got killed.

My boys are still out there fighting. They began as young boys and are now young men…

VERN: …and experienced.

CARLOS: They used to call that little rope *cordarita*.

They've been in this fight for six years. I can't get them out. One is a commandante.

VERN: How did things go when your family came out of Nicaragua?

CARLOS: We went to ACNUR and inquired about help. They only offered to ship us back to Nicaragua. Vladimir was the boss at that time. We received no help from this United Nations Relief Organization.

When the Contras need help with a truck or something, I help. This also keeps my family and myself alive.

VERN: Do most Indians feel that ACNUR works on behalf of the Left?

CARLOS: Yes, they don't have to ask. They can see it! ACNUR works with the "piries," and we all suffer from it.

One of my younger boys, my thirteen-year-old, was hit by lightning last year and is now losing his sight. Though ACNUR has a medical program here, these Communists, as I call them, didn't do anything.

ACNUR propaganda is to get as many as possible back to Nicaragua where the Cubans operate the hospitals. If one gets sick there, it is better to remain at home. The one who walks into their hospital will be brought out dead.

Aircraft loading refugees who have been lured back to Nicaragua by the Sandanistas.

"Bad Sandinista Character Was Not Seen"

VERN: Here in Honduras, Miskitos who are disgusted with the restrictions placed upon them as refugees are leaving on a paid flight to Nicaragua, as I saw them do today in Mocoron under the guidance of ACNUR.

CARLOS: When these refugees left Nicaragua, the bad Sandinista character was not seen the way it is today.

Many things are happening within Nicaragua, but this information often doesn't get out. Only good things are reported, but it is not so.

There was a young neighbor boy who lived over in that house over there [Carlos pointed] who went back with his family to Nicaragua. His name was Hieronymus. The Sandinistas accused him of being a Contra and shot him. He was in school here and didn't want to go to Nicaragua but his parents wanted him to leave with them.

VERN: How old was the boy?

CARLOS: Fourteen.

VERN: How about the reported concentration camps established by the Sandinistas?[1]

CARLOS: These are places that are fenced. There is one near Sahsa. They took many people from the Coco River to this concentration camp. Here they used to bury eight to ten people every day.

People would be cleared out of their villages and forced to walk and sleep in mud. I know about this. The older ones that couldn't walk were left in their houses which were burned. They took children from their mothers and transported them in helicopters to a park in Puerto Cabezas.[2] It was as if you had a whole group of parrots stuck in a cage. They treated these poor crying children in this way. Parents were forced to walk for days until they were picked up by a truck and taken to their children.

People in Honduras don't believe that Communists are that bad. One can see all kinds of writings on the walls of buildings in Tegucigalpa.

VERN: I have heard that Managua started in the same way and now has much graffiti.

CARLOS: If you had seen Managua before and would see Managua now, you would scratch your head. Whatever the Sandinistas touch is ruined.

I am reminded of one of my cousins who had been working with the *piricuacos* and then got away from them. His name was Sebastian Muller. Everyone called him "Smithy." He went with Commandante Zero, Eden Pastora.[3] While bombing an ammunition dump at Augusto Cesar Sandino Airport on September 8, 1983, he was killed with another man, Ramon.[4] The plane flew too low and one wing hit the control tower.[5]

There are plenty of Mullers around doing different things, coward Mullers and those out doing the fighting.

VERN: What is the attitude of Freedom Fighters in general?

CARLOS: In the largest group, the FDN, one can find Sumo and Miskito fighting with them, not only within their own grouping. Indians will get in with any group as long as they are fighting against Communists.

Father Hugh Heinzen.

Father Hugh Heinzen
Puerto Lempira, Gracias A Dios, Honduras
June 18, 1987

Father Hugh Heinzen, Padre Hugo as the Miskitos call him, was born in 1936. A native of Marshfield, Wisconsin, he attended Roman Catholic schools in Wisconsin, Michigan, and Indiana. As a Capuchin[1] priest, he came to Nicaragua's East Coast in 1965 and was expelled by the Sandinistas after having served as a missionary for seventeen years. Five more were spent among many of the same people who became refugees in Honduras.

"Forced to Attend Lectures"

FATHER HEINZEN: From 1965 till 1982 when I went to Puerto Lempira my work had been centered from two Nicaraguan communities, Bluefields and Waspam.

The seven years which I spent in the Bluefields area included work in the following communities: Bluefields; Pearl Lagoon with its thirteen neighboring villages, some which have a Spanish Catholic population; a Spanish ancestry community with some Miskito Indians at Kukra Hill which was near three villages with only Spanish-speaking people; four other villages where only the Miskito language was spoken; and five other communities which used only English.

In 1972 when I began ministering in Waspam, the community contained about one thousand inhabitants. When I was expelled,[2] there must have been about three thousand people there and it was still growing.

In the days of Somoza, it served as a center for the Health, Education, and Commerce offices. When the high school was built, it attracted people to move there.

In April 1981, after the difficulties the Miskito Indians had with the Sandinista takeover, people from a few villages crossed the Coco River. But when the refugees began coming to Mocoron, Honduras, in 1982, they came in droves.

Besides the church in Puerto Lempira, I minister to refugees and Honduran Catholics in Mocoron and twelve Catholic villages near Mocoron.

Last year, I served in the Auka, Honduras, area where there are Honduran Catholics in seven villages plus two refugee villages on the Kruta River.

VERN: What kind of Sandinista activity did you notice before 1979?

FR. HEINZEN: My fellow workers and myself knew that the Sandinista Front existed. Living on the Atlantic Coast, we felt isolated.

VERN: Would you relate some details concerning the terrible action that Sandinistas took against Miskito Indians?

FR. HEINZEN: Bishop Salvador Schlaefer and I were visiting churches in the area of San Carlos which lies along the Coco River some eighty miles west of Waspam. This took place at the end of November and the first part of December 1981

People were talking about their problems with the government. It was typical for Indians to be questioned when they came to town: "Where did you come from? Where are you going?" Townsfolk would be called together in the morning and forced to attend lectures concerning the Revolution; they couldn't go out to their farming duties as they wished.

I ran into some difficulty, as Sandinista soldiers at San Carlos had taken and used my outboard motor while I was gone.

Some days later some fellow priests and I left for a diocese meeting scheduled for the December 13 in Managua. The sisters told us that we shouldn't go because they thought that we wouldn't be coming back for Christmas

Not understanding what they were "picking up," we replied that, of course, we would be coming back for Christmas.

As things turned out, we were successful in returning but with some difficulty. Upon landing in Waspam, I noticed a helicopter situated off to one side with its rotors removed. Men were working on it. It seemed out of place.

A military officer came up to me as I got off the plane and said, "Father, Rufus[3] wants to see you."

"He wants to see me?" I asked.

"No," he answered, "all of the Fathers."

"Where is Rufus?" I asked.

"In Puerto Cabezas."

"All Indians Were Contras"

FR. HEINZEN: We told the sisters that we were leaving, and asked them to inform others that there wouldn't be any Mass in the evening.

The atmosphere at Waspam gave us a hint that ominous things were taking place. Townspeople told us of fighting at San Carlos. This explained the helicopter.

We reached Puerto Cabezas after dark and went to the parish house where we planned to spend the night. Then at the Sandinista headquarters, a secretary said, "Rufus, the Fathers are here."

When he came out, he said, "Gee, I'm awfully busy. Is it all right if I see you, tomorrow?"

"Well, okay. What time?"

"Eight o'clock in the morning."

In the morning we went down to his office which was maybe eight by twelve feet or something like that, a very dinky thing. There was a big desk, some cabinets, no windows, and a double wall which gave us the impression that someone was after him and wanted to shoot him.

We listened as he spoke, "You know that we have problems up on the Coco River. The Contra anti-revolutionaries came over the Coco and killed our troops at San Carlos."

I didn't know what triggered the war. Apparently, a number of young men had gone into Honduras, secured some arms (twenty-two caliber and I heard some bows and arrows) returned, and killed twenty-three soldiers.

Rufus sent a helicopter to San Carlos. While it was landing troops, Miskito boys ambushed it with captured AK-47 rifles. They killed, wounded, and captured a few soldiers. The helicopter pilot was wounded and later died. The co-pilot managed to get the aircraft back to Waspam.

The commandante continued talking about the Sandinista Revolution and emphasizing that what took place at San Carlos couldn't be permitted. He heard that I had said something in San Carlos that he didn't like.

It was true that I had said something about Communism in the San Carlos church. I told the parishioners that Communism was already here.

Finally, as I was getting tired of listening to him, I bluntly asked, "Rufus, what is our role? What do you want us to do?"

"I don't think you can do anything," he replied, but continued talking.

"I suppose you want to return to Waspam?" he finally asked, and our meeting ended. We never did come to a conclusion as to what he wanted. One from our group then said, "We've got to get back for Christmas. The people are expecting us."

Rufus shouted to a couple of his men to get a vehicle and take us back to Waspam and added, "If you can't find one, take my Jeep."

He had a brand new Jeep and we were taken back in that.

On December 22, a large number of people were stopped by troops stationed at Leimus, a small village with about ten families. Many of these men and women worked in Puerto Cabeza and at the gold mines. They were on their way to visit relatives for Christmas in Aasang, San Carlos, Waspuk, Krasa, etc. A few were from the Honduran side of the Coco.

On the night of December 23, the soldiers separated the women from the men. They killed thirty-five men that night and raped the women, whom they then sent on the way to their communities. Later, on the 24th and the 26th, sixteen more were killed. Some were forced into the Coco River. Others were forced to dig their own graves and were buried alive.

At Leimus, twenty miles from Waspam, there was a turpentine company barge which one could use to cross the Coco. Originally, the barge had been utilized to haul stumps out of Honduras into Nicaragua where the turpentine was produced.

Some of the executions took place in connection with this barge, and the bodies eventually floated downriver to a village about five miles west of Waspam. The villagers buried the bodies and then came to us. Though they didn't know where the bodies had come from at first, word was moving fast. The Indians have a terrific telephone system, the "vines of the jungle" we call it.

Christmas and New Year's were sad. Little by little, we began to find out about the many who had been killed and mistreated. Though we fathers did some investigation and got a few names, we eventually left that detail work with our people.

Since I came into Honduras, the record has been compiled. It is now known who was killed and who the Sandinista soldiers were that committed the atrocities. It appears that the soldiers were carrying out an act of revenge for what had happened at San Carlos. To the Sandinistas, all Indians were Contras and those who fell into their hands had to be punished.[1]

Archibald Theofilo.

Archibald Theofilo

Tegucigalpa, Honduras

June 23, 1987

It is tragic that many selfish and irresponsible leaders in the United States Congress are fighting the Freedom Fighters of Central America. Archibald and the Freedom Fighters are not fooled by the lies of the Left.

"Great Economic Strides"

ARCHIBALD: I come from the largest town, Bluefields, on the east-south-east coast of Nicaragua.

VERN: Where did the name Bluefields come from?

ARCHIBALD: As far as I know, some warriors created this name during the time of slavery. We have some high mountains here with many pine, cedar, and mahogany trees.

VERN: Where were you born?

ARCHIBALD: Bluefields, in 1933.

My mother came from Bluefields and my father from Pearl Lagoon, north of Bluefields. The grandfather on my mother's side came from Jamaica. The grandfather on my father's side was Colombian from St. Andreas, an island off the East Coast of Nicaragua. One can find many with the Archibald family name there today.

VERN: You have Creole[1] background?

ARCHIBALD: Yes, though the first of our people that went to Bluefields were slaves from Africa, the first to have lived here were Rama Indians who were followed by the Miskitos.

Today, Blacks are the majority in this area, with approximately, eighty thousand.

VERN: Where did your last name come from?

ARCHIBALD: It comes from the Bible and means "God is love."

VERN: Are all in Bluefields of the Christian faith?

ARCHIBALD: Ninety percent are Protestant, with the largest group being the Moravian Church, whose missionaries had came England. English is the main language spoken in Bluefields.

VERN: What other religious groups are active in Bluefields?

ARCHIBALD: Fifty percent are Moravians and about ten percent are Catholics, the second largest group. There are also Baptists, Church of God, Seventh Day Adventists, Lutherans, and a few others.

VERN: Would you relate a few things about your background?

ARCHIBALD: I'd been on the sea since 1950; I made my first trip to New Orleans as a seventeen- or eighteen-year-old sailor. At that time, Nicaragua was beginning to make great economic strides. It was producing lots of mahogany lumber, different companies were becoming active and busy, and gold was pouring out of the country, 2,500 to 3,000 pounds every month.

Before I fled for my life as a refugee, I had been self-employed for about twenty-five years. I owned a small shrimp boat, two large restaurants, and a furniture shop.

After the Revolution in 1980 there was an American guy who wanted to help East Coast people. Hearing from fellows in Bluefields who mentioned my name, he got in touch with me.

He took a look at my businesses, especially my furniture shop. He felt that I could be of service in preparing young men for a future trade and would give me financial assistance to purchase electrical tools. In addition, he said he would provide my shop with two professional men who would build furniture for export as we had plenty of timber resources nearby. I in turn was to repay this man's money, but only the amount of the loan, interest free.

This was okay with me but we first had to obtain the new government's approval. I spoke to the Bluefields Commandante, Lumberto Campbell, who approved our plans.

In Managua the American gave me thirty thousand *cordobas,* with which I purchased a diesel motor to turn a lumber planer I already owned.

When I left for the East Coast, the American encouraged me to return to Managua in order to select more equipment. But other events came along that set my life on a different course.

VERN: What was the American's name?

ARCHIBALD: I was with this man a couple of days and hadn't familiarized myself with his name before I was sent off to prison.

VERN: Sent off to prison?

ARCHIBALD: The people of Bluefields reacted against Sandinista rule which had promised freedoms and a better way of life than under Somoza.

First to Protest

ARCHIBALD: Bluefields became the first community in Nicaragua to stage a mass protest on September 30, 1980. We had between fifteen and twenty thousand on the street with a manifesto demanding that the Sandinista government comply with their promises and send the Cubans home.

After the third day of the protest, at about four o'clock in the morning, troops were sent in and entered people's homes. A lady of about thirty-five years of age was shot in the leg and later had to have it amputated. Also, 250 demonstrators, including me, were sent to jail.[1] As the Bluefields jailhouse could only hold about ten people at a time, all those arrested were flown to Managua.

VERN: Why the strong feeling against Cubans?

ARCHIBALD: Cubans had been sent into the city along with Russians, Libyans, etc. Every week about 200 to 250 Cubans were brought in beginning in the early part of 1980. They were placed in charge of supervising the few large companies that were operating.

The Sandinistas were very clever in that they brought in only black Cubans. If one didn't speak to them, one wouldn't know they were Cubans speaking only Spanish.

These Cubans were not teachers but military personnel who served within the Moravian School in Bluefields and in other communities. Students protested that they went to school to learn Nicaraguan history and about God and Christ, not Lenin and other Communist leaders.[2]

VERN: The Cubans were teaching atheism.

ARCHIBALD: This is what caused the protest to arise so quickly. There was also discontent because small shops near the homes were being forced to close. As a result families had to stand to receive whatever small portion of food was allotted. Children were taken out of school so they could stand in a food line.

Though we had three or four large companies in the city, most of the population worked at a more independent livelihood by fishing, catching shrimp, cutting wood, etc., and selling their products locally.

Yes, Somoza took away certain resources and, maybe, some other things but did not harm the people physically.

In contrast the Sandinista government came in and completely destroyed what the people had and accused the whole community of failing to support the revolution.

VERN: Is it true that the Sandinistas told the poor that they would be receiving what the rich had?

ARCHIBALD: That's what they were telling the people, "Now, everyone is going to be equal."

What happened? The poor became poorer and were forced to work without pay and food. Everyone reached the conclusion that Communism had come into the community.

VERN: How are they getting along today?

ARCHIBALD: Lots of people in Bluefields are asking, "When are you going to free us from the Communists?" Those working among the Sandinistas are asking the same question. I've been passing these things along to the Freedom Fighters.

Protest Aftermath—Prison

VERN: Let's return to your account of the immediate aftermath of the Bluefields protest of 1980.

ARCHIBALD: The government accused the American who wanted to build up the East Coast as one who was working at counterrevolution. In a Managua prison where I was held, the Cuban commandante began to torture captives so they would be compelled to tell lies about the American. I was the only one to have had any contact with the American. This confused the Cuban. I told him that whatever might be done to me, I would never go against the American who loved Bluefields and wanted to live there.

VERN: Where were you imprisoned?

ARCHIBALD: Several different places. First in Chipote for three months and then about a month among the twenty-seven thousand prisoners at Carcel Modelo.

I was taken to a new building in the area of the prison designed for questioning, solitary confinement, and torture. Though always in the dark,

I could tell the time and days by the frequency of food brought to me, three times per day, and by the guard changes every six hours. In the early morning hours, I could hear other prisoners crying out because of beatings and the electric current running through their bodies.

It didn't take long before the Cuban didn't want to speak with me anymore. I was now subjected to having a fingernail pulled out at around two or three every morning.

VERN: What was used to do this?

ARCHIBALD: Pliers. Now, my nails don't grow. After the second one went, I fainted. I was later pulled out from the cell while a doctor checked me over and gave me an injection and two pills. Then, I was returned to the cell, where I remained for a month and a half before being taken out to where there were many prisoners.

VERN: How long were you in prison?

ARCHIBALD: I came out in August 1981 after ten months. Strange isn't it? Being condemned for five years and then released because nothing could be found against me?

When I returned to Bluefields, the American sent regards and said that because of the situation which he was under, he couldn't assist me anymore.

VERN: Where did he live?

ARCHIBALD: Managua.

VERN: Do you know if he was imprisoned?

ARCHIBALD: I don't know.

Pressure and Escape

ARCHIBALD: I was ordered to join the local CDS or face going back to prison. On certain days I was stuck with the job of making home deliveries to the elderly and the needy. With my delivering their allotments of five pounds of beans, five of flour, and a set amount of oil, I discovered that this "position" had been created so that information about people could be passed on to the government. Agents would come and question me as to what "news" I had for them. I had to make up things.

VERN: How long were you with the CDS?

ARCHIBALD: More or less about six months. In April of '82, Jenelee Hodgson, who spent four or five months in jail under the same circumstances as myself, telephoned me from Costa Rica. She asked if I'd like to cooperate with the Freedom Fighters who just were beginning their operations in our area.

VERN: I have heard of the Hodgson family name.

ARCHIBALD: It's the largest family in Bluefields.

VERN: Do you think that the Sandinistas were listening to your conversation?

ARCHIBALD: Could be. They listen to everything. Anyway, we in Bluefields have a special way of speaking to each other.

I told Jenelee that I'd cooperate.

So a genuine contact could be made, she sent a lady from Costa Rica via Corn Island.

As a result of this connection about thirty Bluefields leaders attended a "birthday party" which I scheduled in June.

VERN: That you were having a party had to be reported to the local CDS?

ARCHIBALD: Yes and to our gathering came a spy, a Spaniard, who couldn't understand our way of speaking.

We were given a working time of three months in Freedom Fighter duty, and we successfully organized several groups. One was in Tasbapauni situated north along the coast about two hours away by speedboat and another in the Turswani River area about an hour south.

Those of us who had gotten involved began planning our escape from the country. In the midst of these considerations, a friend[1] who was employed with the Sandinista Security came to me with timely advice.

"Archibald," he said, "we recognize who you are and what you are trying to do. I advise you to flee from Bluefields as the Sandinistas are about to return you to jail."

Returning to prison would certainly have brought about my death. The following day, I went to Pearl Lagoon where I hid for about eighteen days.

Finally, three men and I who shared the same problem got a dory² with a small sail and went out to sea. The first night brought us into rough weather, and we lost all the food we had brought along. However, three days later we reached Costa Rica safely.

Within six days the Sandinista government found out that I was gone. They went to my house. From the first floor they took everything out of the furniture shop, and from the second all the household goods.

I was informed in prison that the authorities were planning to confiscate the equipment given by the American, so my wife had hidden the lumber planer along with the diesel motor.

VERN: How did the family fare afterwards?

ARCHIBALD: About ten days after I reached Costa Rica, my oldest boy obtained a tourist visa and went out by bus.

Steadman Fagoth found out that I had arrived in Costa Rica and made contact with me. He paid for my passage to Honduras where I began to work with the Miskito Freedom Fighters.

Our second-oldest boy made his way to Managua, took a bus to the northern part of the country, sneaked over the Nicaragua-Honduran border where he was placed in jail, and later was brought to the refugee camp at Teupasenti. When he told camp officials that his father was in Honduras, I was contacted and got him released.

Two more children, Rena and George, both arrived in Honduras in December 1983.

My wife entered Honduras two months later. After a month, she returned to Nicaragua and following another two months left for good.

VERN: All of your children are now out of Nicaragua?

ARCHIBALD: All except one, a son. The Sandinistas had him in prison for over a year. This child was in his teens when I left. He didn't want to come to Honduras, so my wife was forced to leave him. Who knows how the mind of a teenager works sometimes…with the house being plundered and the Sandinistas leaving behind two stereos with thousands of records?

At play on the Rus Rus River.

When officials became aware that I was participating in Freedom Fighting, he was placed in jail. When they asked him to take part in the military, he refused.[3]

East Coast Soviet Base

VERN: The problems in Central America are meshed into American political squabbles. How can Freedom Fighters do a better job in presenting their story?

ARCHIBALD: At the first meeting which we East Coast leaders had in Puerto Cabezas with the Sandinista, Tomas Borge told us that if the new government had to kill every person living on the East Coast in order to make it a Soviet base, it was going to be done.

VERN: When was this?

ARCHIBALD: November 1979. Bluefields had six delegates represented at a meeting of the Miskito organization called ALPROMISO, a name later changed to MISURASATA.

VERN: You were a member of ALPROMISO?

ARCHIBALD: No, I was a member of the Southern Indigenous Creole Community; SICC are the letters of its Spanish title.

When I tell United States people about these sort of things, they don't understand what is happening. Many leaders have known all along that the Sandinista government was Communist but tried to hide this knowledge from the American people.

VERN: Recently the East Coast Freedom Fighters had a meeting where various groups among them met at Rus Rus, Honduras.[1]

ARCHIBALD: They had attempted to get together more than eight times before. It finally became a reality a few weeks ago.

VERN: I have heard that Brooklyn Rivera, the Miskito leader who is fighting the Sandinistas in the southeast section, thinks that he can negotiate with the Communists.

ARCHIBALD: His is a negative attitude! Brooklyn doesn't mind what government might be in charge of Nicaragua, even communistic, as long as the Miskitos receive autonomy.

Americans are interested in making Nicaragua a democratic land where there will be free speech and where its people will be satisfied. Once the Sandinistas are forced out of power and democratic rights are initiated in the handling of products which the area produces, then autonomy can be considered.[2]

As over against what Brooklyn would want,[3] what about the Black people? What about the Sumo and the Rama Indians? What about the Ladino people who are the majority of the people of Nicaragua in the western regions? All these should be considered as having rights, too.

Steadman Fagoth and Wycliffe Diego are Miskito Indians who have a different approach than Brooklyn. These leaders want autonomy, but first they want to get rid of the Communists.

I pray that Brooklyn and Fagoth can work together and do the right thing for the future of our children.

VERN: Does Brooklyn have a majority of blacks among his troops?

At Rus Rus, Gracias a Dios, in Honduras, delivering products.

Section of the medical complex in Rus Rus, Gracias a Dios, Honduras.

ARCHIBALD: Yes.

VERN: I assume that these men and women think the way that you do?

ARCHIBALD: Exactly. We Creoles feel that we are also a part of Nicaragua but are willing to allow democracy to take its course. With Communists, one is dealing with liars who cannot be believed nor trusted.

VERN: How about Jenelee? Is she working with Brooklyn?

ARCHIBALD: Though it was through her that the Creoles were participating with Brooklyn, she left him because he was constantly attempting to negotiate with the Sandinistas.

VERN: He lost lots of black support?

ARCHIBALD: The situation reached such a point among his troops, and he knew it, that all had to make a special effort to cooperate in order to succeed.[4]

VERN: Within the States your job will be one of public relations?

ARCHIBALD: Yes, this will be my job as soon as we set up a black people's organization like the Miskitos have theirs. We must all work together. Freedom Fighters do not belong to a well-structured military organization. They take up arms because of what Sandinistas have been doing to a family or a friend. As the fighters also have their intelligence sources, these things plus the larger general actions become a part of the civil strife and warfare.

On the other hand, the Sandinistas are better structured militarily. They do similar things to the civilian population but in a more vast and worse manner. They even use a method in which they dress their soldiers in Freedom Fighter uniforms, send them into a village to commit wrongs, and then blame the Contras.

In 1983 the Sandinistas destroyed a whole village. They burned down the church and shot and killed its people except for one member. Though hit in the lungs, he escaped into Honduras and reached Tegucigalpa. The Sandinistas were dressed as Freedom Fighters, but he knew who they were because he recognized the commandante as the man in charge of Puerto Cabezas.

VERN: Was his name Rufus?

ARCHIBALD: Rufus! Yes. We told the Americans about this, but they still don't give proper support for our cause.

VERN: Among the Freedom Fighters, this has been an important assignment for you.

ARCHIBALD: Yes, it comprises all of the work which I have been attempting to do. I've been making about seven trips a year to the States.

VERN: I am aware of the fact that not too long ago, last year, you were with President Reagan at a press conference where Secretary of State George Schultz was also in attendance.

ARCHIBALD: I had to touch some very important issues.

Civil War Commitment

VERN: The President is very interested in assisting you.

ARCHIBALD: Oh yes, if we had two more such as he, Nicaragua would be raising Christian flags, already!

VERN: Would you make some statements regarding the Christian commitment of the Freedom Fighters?

ARCHIBALD: One of the important principles of my life is to be involved in Christian activities. I love these things and know Christian churches should be made aware of what is going on.

Eighty percent of East Coast fighters are religious. This I know because I work with them. They believe in God and that He exists "…His wonders to perform." When they go to battle, they pray to the Lord. With most of them, one will find a New Testament supplemented with the Psalms and Proverbs in either Spanish or English.

Most of the Creoles use either those in English or in Spanish. The Miskitos usually use the Spanish translations. A lady from Texas had donated thousands of these with the FDN Freedom Fighters getting them also.

VERN: I notice the New Testaments, with this on the first page, "Righteousness exalted a nation, but sin is a reproach to any people." (Proverbs 14:34), come from the Gideons. Besides the scripture itself, each contains familiar hymns, extra helps and Bible references where one can receive aid in various kinds of situations. There are also passage listings pertaining to virtue and character.

ARCHIBALD: The fighters pray every morning. Their service is conducted from 5:30 to 6:30.

VERN: Are there chaplains among them?

ARCHIBALD: No, they have a prayer service and read scripture with some commentary. Accustomed as they were to worship this way in their home communities, so in exile and in their fighting duties they continue to honor their Lord.

VERN: On the East Coast, it appears as if your political life is part and parcel with your religious life.

ARCHIBALD: Right.

VERN: Do the Ladino Freedom Fighters have prayer time?

ARCHIBALD: They have worship time just as the Indians and the blacks have. Most are Catholics. I don't know of priests among the FDN fighters, but I do know a Ladino Protestant preacher who lives with them. Many are the fighters who didn't know the Lord but who do now, as in any conflict.

VERN: What was Somoza like when it came to encouraging religious life on the East Coast?

ARCHIBALD: Somoza invested in Nicaragua. One could go to Somoza and whatever religion one belonged to, one could always get a message through to him. If there was needed a church to be built, say, in Bluefields, he would help. Lots of money was invested in this way on the East Coast. There was hardly a location where one could travel and find a school and a church that had not been placed there by Somoza. He was not as bad as many had painted him.

We tried to get something better in Nicaragua, but should have done it in a democratic way, not in a revolution which turned out to be many times worse than Somoza ever was.

Under him the people of Bluefields were beginning to benefit. Besides government salaries given to public school teachers, he granted certain sums to teachers in private schools, such as the Moravian School. Things were beginning to improve when we "fell down into a hole."

Ruth Lissa de Castillo and daughter, Lisbet, who saved Ruth's life.

Ruth Lissa Gasden de Castillo

Tegucigalpa, Honduras

July 29, 1987

Knowing that the followers of Communism were bent on destroying all that this brave lady considered right, she revealed a part of what she did. Ruth spent six years of self-giving heroism among the Contras.

"My Mama Gone Managua"

VERN: Would you give some information as to your background?

RUTH: In 1975 I got married at fifteen years of age. My husband was thirty-seven. Though he had been an average government employee, someone later accused him of working with the Somocistas, and he was imprisoned for one year. A friend got him to the States in 1981.

VERN: You also hope, I assume, to reach the States?

RUTH: A few days ago, I had telephone contact with him.

VERN: How long had it been since you spoke with him?

RUTH: Whew! Four or five years. I'm certainly hoping something can be worked out. With my husband gone, I remained single and dedicated myself to work with the Freedom Fighters in 1981.

Let's look at the 1983-84 period of time in which I helped carry food, various other supplies, messages, and people by means of a small dory of a type used along coastal waters called a "tuk-tuk." The name corresponds to the sound of its small engine.

Coming and going to a Contra base south of Bluefields on this boat were usually myself and two companions: Vilma and her husband Marcus, who have both fled to Costa Rica.

In Bluefields I had a sewing machine with which to make some money for my daughter, Lisbet, and myself and to pay the helper who took care of Lisbet when I was gone.

The helper, a Sumo Indian lady, came from a village where she witnessed the Sandinista execution of one of her nephews. With her assistance, I could get into the bush for a time.

163

On one occasion as I was about to leave on one of these clandestine trips, I accidentally revealed to my daughter that I was leaving.

She immediately inquired, "Mama, where you going?"

Without thinking I answered, "To the bush."

"Going to leave for the boys?"

"Yes."

I forgot about this conversation until we reached our Contra camp destination, a place called Jally in the vicinity of Rama Key. When I remembered what I had done, I told my friend, "Vilma! I told Lisbet that I was going into the bush. If the Sandinistas come to the house in search of me, she might tell them!"

Vilma answered with alarm, "Why did you do it?"

Thinking about it made me sick.

When we returned to Bluefields, my helper related how a State Security man named Leonel Borge had indeed come looking for me. Though she was at the back of the house, she heard Lisbet tell him, "My mama gone Managua!"

Peeping through a back wall, she observed Lisbet speaking with a man outside the house. She could watch him as he was framed by a front window. She heard the official inquire, "Where is your mama?"

"My mama gone Managua!"

"You sure she went to Managua?"

"She went buy food."

My helper was very frightened when Lisbet ran into the house as the man was leaving and announced, "Sandinista come for my mama, but I tell, 'My mama gone Managua.'"

VERN: How old was Lisbet at this time?

RUTH: About four years. My dear Sumo friend became so nervous that she bathed Lisbet, placed fresh clothes on her, and took her out for a walk.

Meeting some dear friends, Lisbet suddenly, exclaimed, "Mama gone! She gone to Contras, them."

Quickly, one of the friends quietly said, "No, darling, don't say that so people may hear. All in your house could go to jail!"

She responded with, "Sandinista with two pistols won't find Mama!"

Now, alarmed, the friend asked, "What did you tell him?"

"I tell, 'My mama gone Managua!'"

The friend swept her up into his arms and kissed her.

When I heard about it, I spoke to Lisbet and we discussed the affair.

The experience was followed by two Contra missions, one of fifteen days duration and the other in which I was forced to remain in the bush for twenty-three days. There had been a military engagement, and I had to see to it that children in the area of combat were taken to a wooded place with adequate bomb shelters.

I couldn't return sooner because I became sick with a severe cold. The paramedics took care of me until I felt better.

While I was gone, the Sandinista Security man came again to the house. This time he came with candy for Lisbet, and a pair of trousers that needed repair. "Lisbet, where is your mama?" he asked.

"My mama gone Managua!"

"What is your mama doing there?"

"She sells things."

VERN: Had you coached Lisbet as to what to say?

RUTH: My helper did. The Security agent gave Lisbet the candy and asked when her mama would be returning.

Lisbet replied, "I don't know when Mama coming."

"When she comes back, " he said kindly, "I will return."

Three days later he returned and asked, "Your mama don't come?"

"No" was her answer.

Giving her more candy, he continued, "Do you know your mama carries food for the Contras? Right now, she is in the bush and hasn't returned."

Lisbet quickly answered, "No, my mama not in bush," and ran inside the house.

As her helper came outside, the officer said dryly, "Hmm, you're with this child. What are you doing here?"

"Her mama went to Managua, so she asked me to mind her baby."

"You're all colleagues in this matter!" the officer said sharply. "You're all one with the Contras!"

Because of the recent combat, a problem developed of which my companions and I were not aware. Martial law had been declared in Bluefields.

As we approached the city in our small boat, I felt insecure. It was about six o'clock in the evening and dark and raining.

With no warning, automatic rifle fire fell upon us, narrowly missing our motorized canoe. We thought we were going to die, but God saved us. W turned the boat around and made for one of the small keys called Key Pigeon. We hid inside this key as a Coast Guard patrol vessel passed back and forth. After it left, we remained in hiding till about four in the morning.

At six, when we saw fishing boats about, we asked some of the fishermen if it was all right to enter Bluefields. They indicated that we could go in.

Although I remained ill, I was advised not to go to the doctor because he was Cuban.

The following evening at about six, there was a knock at the door. Our helper went to check.

It was a Security official. "Ruth come?"

"No," my house aide answered, "she hasn't come yet."

"Someone told me she had come back."

"We went down to the wharf, but she hadn't returned. Probably tomorrow."

Suspiciously, he said, "Hmm, something is funny."

The next day, I was still not feeling well. Vilma came over and said, "Ruthie, they came to my house looking for you. Let's make a move to Managua!"

The following morning we hired a speedboat from Bluefields to Rama, about two and a half hours away. Then from there it took another four to five hours by bus.

Vilma and I stayed in Managua a month.

VERN: Was your little girl along?

RUTH: Yes. Later, back in Bluefields,we went about our business as usual.

"Mommy! Mommy! Sandinista Coming!"

VERN: Where was your home town?

RUTH: Puerto Cabezas.

I consider myself a mixed-blood with my mother tongue being English. The grandfather on my father's side was English, and my grandmother was a mixed-blood from Belize.[1]

On my mother's side, my grandfather was black and came from Jamaica. My grandmother had Miskito and Spanish heritage.

My husband's grandfather on his mother's side was from America. His grandmother was Spanish. The family on his father's side was of Spanish heritage.

VERN: Did you ever return to Puerto Cabezas after your '83-'84 experience in Bluefields?

RUTH: Yes, in 1985, but didn't stay long as the authorities had their eyes on me.

In '86, I was in Managua but kept moving from place to place such as Corn Island, Kukra, Corinto, and so forth.

Once when I returned to Puerto Cabeza, relatives informed me that the government wanted to seize Jimmy, my sixteen-year-old nephew, for the armed forces. His parents didn't want this.

The government forced young boys into service, gave them ten days of basic training, and then sent them against the Freedom Fighters.

Giving Jimmy a woolen shirt and a cap, I left Port with him and my daughter who was then six years old. We boarded a truck used for carrying passengers. We hoped to reach Honduras.

At Bismuna the truck driver dropped us off at a house by the creek where we remained three days and three nights without going outside. At an earlier time, the lady of the house, a Miskito, had been expelled from her home and sent to Puerto Cabezas, where I had become acquainted with her and assisted her. Now, she was caring for my needs.

I tried to figure out a way to reach Cabo Gracias a Dios, which would have meant freedom for us. Though this area was in Nicaragua, it was in the hands of the Freedom Fighters. Nicaraguan citizens who lived there were able to move back and forth into Nicaragua as long as they had proper documents. Jimmy, Lisbet, and I did not possess documents.

After three days, I asked our hostess if I could attend evening services at the local Moravian church. It was in the midst of a conference of the surrounding congregations.

"Okay," she replied, "go!"

The church was lit by a large Coleman lamp, and I sat in a position where the light allowed me to read the hymnbook clearly. I was enjoying the worship service when, suddenly, a Sandinista Security officer stared through a window directly at me. He was a mixed-blood, Miskito and Spanish, whose name was Dublon.

He frightened me, and yet I had to make my way back to the lady's house. It is possible that I was followed.

In the morning Lisbet was standing at the halfway, open door of the house, Jimmy was lying on one bed, I in another, and the house owner was combing her hair.

All of a sudden, Lisbet exclaimed, "Mommy, Mommy! Sandinista coming!"

Six soldiers quickly entered the house. One of them, Dublon, ordered, "Don't move!" To reinforce the command, he walked over to Jimmy, who had gotten up, and roughly pushed him back to his mat.

Then he said to Jimmy, "Ah, I've seen you fighting at the San Juan River. He's a Contra!"

I stood up and exclaimed, "No, Sandinista, Jimmy is not a Contra!"

He looked at me and said sternly, "Yes, he is, and you are a Contra too! I've been trailing you."

The elderly lady jumped into the midst of our argument and added, "No, no! When you forced us out to Puerto Cabezas, this little boy fished so we could eat. If you're going to kill this boy, you can kill all of us!"

Dublon looked at me and ordered, "I want your names!"

I told him, "Ruth Butt…Jimmy," and looking straight at Lisbet while she watched me, I said, "Lisset."

A lieutenant, an assistant to Dublon, then went to Lisbet and asked her in Spanish, "What is your name?"

Curtly, she answered in Spanish, "Just how my mama tell."

She speaks three languages: English, Miskito, and Spanish.

"But your Mama gave your name as Lisset. Is this true?"

"*Si, mi amo Lisset*" ["Yes, my name is Lisset."]

Dublon interrupted, "No, Lisbet!"

My heart went boom!

Lisbet persisted: "No, my name is Lisset, just how my mommy tell you my name!"

"Praise God!" were the silent words that came out of me.

Dublon took our names down and announced, "I will be calling Puerto Cabezas. You will report to the post at six this evening."

I reacted, "Six o'clock! No, I don't go out in the night."

Dublon haughtily replied, "Ha, ha, what is this? You'll do what we say!"

"Okay," I answered, "I'll go.

On the way to the base, I met a lady and said to her, "Please accompany me to the headquarters of the commandante."

Alarmed, she spoke softly, "Oh, don't go there! Everyone strange in the neighborhood is immediately suspected of wanting to cross into Honduras. There is a boat leaving before they come out of the post." Pointing in the direction where the boat was, she whispered, "Run to the boat, this way!"

VERN: When did this scene take place?

RUTH: The first of March. I told the lady that if I didn't go, the officer said he would lock me up.

As I continued alone up the hill toward the post, I heard the "click, click" of the safety lock of a pistol, accompanied by the command, "Stand still! Don't move!"

Dublon came up to me, took hold of my dress at the chest, and announced, "You are a Contra!"

My immediate response was, "No!"

"I've gotten information on you from Port and I'm sending you there tomorrow. You are a Contra. You're heading for Honduras and to the Contras there. That wish you're not going to have. But, if you lie with me, I won't send you to jail."

"No!"

"The Contras shall not get you," he responded, and held his pistol to my head, forcing me to the ground.

I fought him and he struck me.

When I told Dublon that I was a Christian and what he wanted was a sin which I could not enter into, he laughed and said, "This word, 'Christian,' is just a name Contras like to use. It's all politics. What kind of a Christian are you?"

Then he beat and raped me.

Later, I shoved him out of my way and ran down to the boat owner, the one I had been directed to earlier. I pleaded, "Before you leave, will you please take me aboard?"

Shaking his head sadly, he said with sympathy, "I want you to come aboard, but Dublon will come and ask if I transported you and the two children. He will say, 'If that woman disappears from this place, you will drop dead!'"

The boat owner suggested that we get a dory and do what had to be done. He, meanwhile, would be going back to Port.

I had gotten myself into a mess and was worried. But then I found out that Dublon had been called out of Bismuna early that morning to fight the Contras, who had made an attack at the neighboring village of Wasla.

At five that same morning, the lady I was staying with urged, "Run! See if the boatman is still here."

The boat was already gone, so the children and I returned to the house.

At about eight o'clock, I went to the military base and inquired, "Who is the official in command?"

A lieutenant stepped up and answered, "Me."

"Hello."

"Hello, you aren't from this village?"

"No, I'm from Cabo Gracias A Dios."

"I've never known there were any pretty girls from that place."

"Yes, I've been living in Managua, but I want to visit my mama who is coming from Honduras. You all say that we should have autonomy and be free."

"Come to the headquarters at eleven tonight."

This officer, a second in command, hadn't seen me before, nor did he know that Jimmy was with me. I felt that I had to meet with him, hopefully to win our freedom into Honduras.

This man was waiting for me but not at the base. Leaving his bodyguard at a distance, he met me about a half block from the post. From behind a tree, he announced, "I received the report on you and can't let you pass to Cabo Gracias a Dios. Lie with me and I'll let you go, but not with your daughter."

"If you don't let me take my daughter, forget it. I'm going," I said and began moving from him.

Grabbing me from behind and holding me by my dress, he kicked with his foot so I tripped and fell. Then he raped me.

Afterward, I pushed him aside, but he held on to me and said, "If you want to go, leave your daughter with me. If you take her, you and I know that you won't return."

As I had hidden Jimmy in the boat earlier, I finally agreed to leave Lisbet at the house of my friend in Bismuna and got permission to travel to

Cabo Gracias a Dios. There I was to meet and accompany my mother to Puerto Cabezas.

At four in the morning, I was on my way with Jimmy and returned at eleven.

Early the next morning I was on my way to Puerto Cabezas with Lisbet. There, a Security officer said, "I have been informed that you have been to Honduras."

"No," I said, "I went to Managua and just now have come back. People are talking lies. What would I want to go to Honduras for?"

"Refugees Are Contras and Are Nobody!"

A friend looked for a way for me to get away from Port. Securing the services of a man with a dory who wanted 150,000 *cordobas*, I told him that I didn't have that much, only 45,000.

The friend, urging the man, said, "Please, take her out. I'll figure a way to repay afterwards."

The man took me.

The boatman left me at Sandy Bay at two o'clock in the morning while he visited other places in that area. Returning five hours later, he took me to Cabo Gracias a Dios. We arrived at five in the afternoon.

After about fifteen days at the Cabo, the Freedom Fighters took me to Iralaya, Honduras. There I stayed about three months before becoming very, very ill. A Nicaraguan whose fighting name was Mr. Donkey took me to a doctor in Puerto Lempira whose care made me feel a little better.

I went to live at the home of one of my cousins whom I hadn't known before. She did her best to help Lisbet, Jimmy, and myself, but her husband, a Honduran, didn't want us. He didn't like Nicaraguans, and things got to such a point that he told his wife that if she continued to aid us, he would bring no more food.

We had a problem. But pleased to be free from Sandinista hands, I felt better about facing this new challenge. So I took the children to another home where a lady gave us lodging.

Three days later I went to see the restaurant owner Marina in Puerto Lempira who gave me work.

I did baking for three days. When she asked me to cook, I cooked. I cleaned the sewage. Whatever she asked of me, I did.

After a month on the job, my little girl got sick. I spoke to my employer, "Miss Marina, my baby got sick. I want to leave until she gets better."

"No, no," she hurriedly said, "you can't leave until I get someone else to take your place."

"Okay," I consented, "I'll do that."

A Honduran army officer visited the restaurant one Sunday that I had made a nice, grated cazaba[1] cake. I did my part in serving his party during the meal.

The officer looked at me from head to foot and saw that I was nice to look at. But then he said, "I wonder which of these waitresses are Nicaraguans?"

One after the other, Marina pointed out those who were Honduran. Then she came to me and said, "The good-looking girl is Nicaraguan."

The officer stood up and declared, "Nicaraguan? All of you belong in a refugee camp. You have no business in Puerto Lempira." Slapping his hand on the table, he shouted, "Right now! Get out!"

Marina intervened and pleaded, "No, no, please do me the favor. She works very well with me. Don't send her where she will suffer. Here, she works and receives a little help."

"Okay, for your sake, she will stay," he declared.

The next day an American couple came to eat, and I did my best to attend to their needs. Everything was in proper order until Marina shouted at me to clean up some sewage, belittling me in front of the Americans.

When the couple left, I said, "Miss Marina, please don't ill-treat me."

"You Nicaraguan refugees are Contras and are nobody!" she snapped.

With this I wept and then said, "Thank you. Today is yours. Tomorrow shall be for myself." As I had more on my mind, I persisted, "In Nicaragua, we weren't treated like this. Because of the Sandinistas we have been placed in a punishing situation. But, mind you, if these same Communists came to Honduras, you would leave your house and run just as I have had to do. So, thank you and pay me my wages."

"I'm not paying you," came the stubborn reply.

"Okay, then, I'll leave you now."

As she didn't even want to hand me the money she had decided to give me, she gave it to someone else to pass it on to me.

Counting it and realizing that she had paid only for ten days work, I protested, "You owe me for a month's work."

"If you want what you have, take it or leave it."

I knew the type and said, "Okay, Mom, thank you. I'll take it and leave you in God's hands."

"Don't talk to me anymore or I'll call the police," she said. "They'll lock you up because you're illegal."

Mr. Archibald Theofilo met me when I first came into Honduras, but he was not able to give me any assistance.

Meanwhile, because of the relationship with Marina, I was forced to go across the lagoon from Puerto Lempira to Pruhmnitara, a refugee area which is next to the ocean.

Though I was away from the terrible conditions of Nicaragua, I felt that I was being given a very rough time by the people of Honduras. I began crying and saying to myself such things as, "I am suffering too much here. I would rather die in Nicaragua. Though the Sandinistas might kill me for getting Jimmy out and though I might have to stand trial, I will do it."

Again, God helped me out as Archibald Theofilo never forgot me and got me out of Prumnitara at a time when I was really suffering.

"Don't Like the Moravian Church"

VERN: On the subject of the Moravian Church, have some pastors been talked into going in with the Sandinistas?[1]

RUTH: They are forced to do it just to keep the church going, but those leaders whom I have known prayed when they wanted to, no matter if they were told not to.

The Sandinistas do not like the Moravian Church. Just this past February, a Moravian Bishop, Andy Shogreen, was tortured by the Sandinistas.

Sandinistas do not like the religious emphasis and prefer their own teaching about fighting the enemy, the Americans. But when children return home at the end of the day, parents correct the children. The Sandinistas can't put it over on the people.

In Puerto Cabezas the only church school open at this time is the Adventist School. When I left, the government was attempting to take it over, also.

VERN: The people of Nicaragua are for the Contras?

RUTH: Yes, the people of Nicaragua are solidly in accord with the Contras. However, they can't do much for them and are forced to stick close to their own families. No one can be trusted.

I would like to go back and do my part. My feelings want to go, but my body is weak. I would like to serve with the last bit of my energy. The missions I had were dangerous, but I was not afraid to do my part.

VERN: I have heard that the Contras have prayer every morning.

RUTH: Before going into battle or on patrol, they have a prayer time. Their favorite Psalm is 146. During training, they pray and then are off to their military exercises. These men serve the Lord. All go to Prayer Time which is from 5:30 to 6:30 every morning.

Thank God I have been kept safe even when the enemy, the Sandinistas, were trying to catch me.

VERN: Some girls were caught?

RUTH: Many! Plenty, all over Nicaragua, and the Sandinistas don't respect women.[2] As for myself, even though I was raped, I still keep to my road as a Christian.

VERN: The Lord continue to bless you in your future.

Afterword

The refugees of Nicaragua have been mentioned but cursorily in the daily news of America's fifty states. In contrast, those who have spoken in the pages of this work have to be considered a primary source of encouragement which North Americans need.

Though the truth of what has happened to these displaced persons seems to be purposely hidden from view,[1] they are aware that the prime country for the forces of the Left to conquer is the United States. They know how their nation's children are taught to hate America in the words of the ruling government's party anthem, "…we will fight the Yankee, For he is the enemy of humanity."[2]

To cover its evil designs, the sinister Nicaraguan leadership points lying fingers, blaming others for its troubles.[3] At the same time it works to shift the field of battle to where it knows it may win, the internal politics of the United States.[4] Tomas Borge Martinez, the Nicaraguan Minister of the Interior, who has been called "the master of unsolved murders,"[5] elucidates this fact in the 1983 *Newsweek* magazine article which stated, "The battle for Nicaragua is not being waged in Nicaragua. It is being fought in the United States."[6]

Repugnant was the Democratic Party's leadership in their "Off Again-On Again" attitude toward the Freedom Fighters of Nicaragua.[7] Liberal Republicans should also be considered in tune with this same cast of characters. Odious actions were taken in their totally irresponsible witch hunt to determine if their unjust legalities hitting these Freedom Fighter friends of America were kept by a just president. (In Bible times, such immoral politics were practiced against the Prophet Daniel.[8])

Another sign of the battle to which Borge referred appears as one examines the spirit and content of TV programing. For the many instances in which names associated with the Left are heard, is there anyone who simply and truthfully explains what is going on in such places as Cuba, with its thirty-year Communist rule, and Nicaragua?

Despite massive infusion of aid, at the beginning of 1989 Nicaragua was numbered among the twentieth-century nations that have suffered the worst inflation. Something worse is yet to come.

Controlling and equipping the largest armed force ever organized within Central America, confiscating businesses and farms, forcing the populace into collectives, assassinating many and selectively detaining others, and promoting restrictive controls for that society have all contributed to general malaise and economic shambling.

The need for freedom in Nicaragua is urgent and great will the United States be if it is able to assist this country and its neighbors.

Notes

Introduction

1. The largest student-operated newspaper in the United States quotes a higher percentage. Joe Roche, "Sandinista Repressing Church in Nicaragua," *The Minnesota Daily,* Friday, Oct. 23, 1987, 7.

On January 16, 1989, "The Caribbean Report" of the radio broadcast of the Voice of America stated in its "United States Administration Editorial" that an estimated 100,000 Nicaraguan refugees had entered the United States in 1988.

The president of Costa Rica, Oscar Arias Sanchez, has recently said that 250,000 refugees have come into his country. Costa Rica contains 23,000 square miles and a population of about two million.

The number of people who have left Nicaragua because of the Sandinista takeover is estimated by Dr. Bernard Nietschmann, a geography professor at the University of California at Berkeley, to even be as high as 700,000 people. This number includes a possible 150,000 in California and Florida.

Cf. "Immigration Rules are Eased for Nicaraguan Exiles in U.S.," *New York Times,* Thurs., July 9, 1987, L-A8.

2. U. S. Department of State, *Human Rights in Nicaragua Under the Sandinistas—From Revolution to Repression,* 5, n. 4—"Press reports indicate that as many as 500,000 Nicaraguans have fled their country since 1979." (Washington, D.C., Dec. 1986)

Jaime Daremblum, "Costa Rica Responds to the Enemy Within," *Wall Street Journal,* Fri., June 14. 1985, 25.

Vince and Ann Magnotta, "Costa Rica's Literacy Boom," *Christian Science Monitor,* Fri., Nov. 1, 1985, 31.

Robert J. McCartney, "Waiting in Honduras: Nicaraguans Fleeing War and Draft Form Support Base for Guerrillas," *Washington Post,* Fri., Sept. 6, 1985, A1.

Stephen Kinzer, "Nicaragua Men Fleeing Draft Fill Honduran Refugee Camp," *New York Times,* Thurs., April 11, 1985, A1.

Nancy Nusser, "Nicaragua's Uprooted Indians," *Christian Science Monitor,* Fri., July 26, 1985, 16.

George Volsky, "Group Would Aid Nicaraguans Here," *New York Times,* Wed., Aug. 28, 1985, A11.

Michael Novak, "Illusions About Nicaragua," *National Review,* Fri., June 29, 1984, 38.

David Maraniss, "In the Valley: The Sanctuary House," *Washington Post,* Wed., Nov. 20, 1985, A1.

Book I—Citizens of Western Nicaragua
Zaida Rodriguez vda de Ortiz

1. In the present Nicaraguan civil war, Santiago fought with the largest group countering the Sandinista government. This organization, called the Nicaraguan Democratic Force (FDN = Fuerza Democratica Nicaraguense), was founded in 1982. Read their "Principles," edited by Robert S. Leiken and Barry Rubin, *The Central American Crises* (New York: Summit Books, 1987), 261-263. At the time of Santiago's death, the FDN numbered about 15,000 men and women and was made up mainly of Ladinos who have Indian and Spanish ancestry, speak Spanish, and are native to the western half of the country. In 1988, there may have been 18,000 FDN Freedom Fighters.

Today, the umbrella organization for the largest group is known as the Nicaraguan Resistance and includes the FDN, the southern group, and others. In fact, there are fifteen or more different names that have been used which are now part of the history within the Nicaraguan Resistance. One of these had twenty members. Another with eighty included two men who were arrested and apprehended in the San Francisco, California, area in connection with illegal cocaine sales. These two men, out of the thousands of Freedom Fighters, made it possible for the press to harass the honorable.

Cf. Christopher Dickey, *With the Contras* (New York: Touchstone-Simon & Schuster, 1987), 115-120

Cf. U.S. Department of State and Department of Defense. *The Challenge to Democracy in Central America* (Washington, D.C., June 1986), 37-46.

2. This name comes from the title, Sandinista National Liberation Front (FSLN = Frente Sandinista de Liberacion Nacional), a Marxist-Leninist guerrilla-terrorist group that seized government power in Nicaragua in July 1979.

3. On the United States national scene, reports were received that the Contras had killed two hundred Nicaraguan soldiers and six prisoners were captured. In contrast to this, the Honduran press reported over three times that number. One of the Tegucigapla Spanish newspapers, *La Tribuna,* stated on Monday, March 31, 1986, that the Nicaraguan Army had gone ten kilometers into Honduras and that seven hundred Sandinista soldiers had been killed by the Honduran army. As the Honduran army participated in the ambush, the country's political leadership invited news media from all over the world to witness what had happened. However, some reports toned down the story. Cf. James Le Moyne, "U.S. Copters Reported Ready to Ferry Troops to the Border Area," *New York Times,* Wed., March 26, 1986, p, L-A1. Cf. Stephen Kinzer, "Nicaragua Denies Its Troops Invaded Honduras," *New York Times,* Wed., March 26, 1986, L-A6.

Another Tegucigalpa Spanish newspaper, *El Hearldo,* on Sat., May 3, 1986, reported on the tension with its headline, "In these Last Months More Than 50 Hondurans Have Died

Because of The 'Nica' Military Situation [trans]." The accompanying article stated that thousands of Hondurans in the area of Nueva Palestina and places within the department of Olancho had to flee in order to save their lives.

4. Utilizing as their example and namesake Augusto Cesar Sandino, a revolutionary executed in the 1930s who condoned mutilation of live people in his attempt to instill terror in the hearts and minds of citizens, the Sandinistas work very hard with the men and women whom they train in attempting to instill a spirit which makes it easy to do any type of savage act.

5. This name is associated with a family in whose hands lay the political power of Nicaragua from about 1936—cf. Bernard Diederich. *Somoza* (New York: E.P. Dutton, 1981), 19-20. The last family member in power, President Anastasio Somoza Debayle, fled the country on July 17, 1979—cf. op. cit., 315-316—and was later assassinated in Paraguay on September 17, 1980. On October 1 of the same year, Paraguay officially severed relations with Nicaragua, citing it had uncovered "irrefutable evidence" of Sandinista involvement. See Facts on File, "Paraguay Breaks Relations" (New York: Facts On File, Inc.: Fri., Oct. 17, 1980), 792—B2.

6. However, during Christmas of 1986, a major American network TV correspondent obliged Sandinista disinformation methods by relating on American television that the Nicaraguan government was allowing its soldiers to return to their homes for Christmas. In 1987 the Sandinistas announced a cease-fire in certain areas at Christmas time, a figment of someone's imagination?

7. The Sandinista Defense Committee (Comite de Defensa Sandinista) is a civilian paramilitary organization which in cities and towns is based upon the residential block with comparable grouping in the rural areas. An important tool for ideological indoctrination, economic and social control of a population, and security enforcement at the local neighborhood level, the CDS under the guise of enlisting volunteers is used as a means of spying on neighborhoods. The organization is a carbon copy of the Cuban model, the Committee for the Defense of the Revolution (CDR = Comite de Defensa Revolucion). Cf. U.S. Department of State, *Human Rights in Nicaragua Under The Sandinistas* ..., op cit., 14.

8. The *cordoba* is the bank monetary unit of Nicaragua. The Black Market exchange rate for the summer of 1986 was approximately 3,000 *cordobas* for one United States dollar.

9. Cf. Fredy Gadea Zeledon (Commandante Coral) and Armando Centeno (Commandante Antonio), "Propuesta De Ayuda Humanitaria," (En Algun Lugar de Nicaragua: Para el Comando Regional Quilali, Resistencia Nicaraguense: April 26, 1988), 9—Nicaraguan refugees in Honduras not cared for by the United Nations but by the Freedom Fighters themselves total at least 20,910 people representing 3,473 families. These were found at the following locations: San Andres, Chiminca, La Bruja, Yamales, Danli, and El Paraiso. [Note: Not included in this count are Miskito refugees in eastern Honduras.]

10. Cf. Steven V. Roberts, "Lawmakers Say New Raid Will Help Cause Of Contras," *New York Times,* Wed., March 26, 1986, L-A6.

Bayardo Antonio Santeliz

"Parasites of the Revolution"

1. Cf. "Reagan's Night for the Refugees—At Fund Raising Dinner, Voices From Nicaragua," *Washington Post,* Tues., April 16, 1985, C1.

2. An eruption of this volcano in 1902 may have been the reason why there is a Panama Canal and not a comparable waterway through Nicaragua today.

3. A Latin American who may farm his own small acreage of land, work on someone else's, or do both.

4. See video still photo of Bayardo in videocassette clip actually including location shooting of the partially burned church. "Oliver North Fight for Freedom" (American Freedom Coalition, Washington, D.C., 1987).

5. By the summer of 1988, the two camps at Jacaleapa, the one at Teupasenti, and a new one at Las Vegas de Jalan begun in the summer of 1987 and located about five miles northeast of Teupasenti, together, would contain a population estimated at 16,000 men, women and children. Housing Nicaraguan refugees, mainly from the north sections of western Nicaraguan, these camps were set up in the general vicinity of Danli by a United Nations organization. A fourth one was set up in the Teupasenti area by 1989.

In an easterly direction from Danli, another refugee camp for Nicaraguan refugees was set up at Yamales for approximately 10,000 already there after a Sandinista attack into Honduras. Cf. *Facts On File,* "Nicaragua Launches Border Offensive" (Fri., March 11, 1988), 177.

Introduction by President Reagan

1. "How to Handle Nicaragua," *Newsweek*, Mon., April 29, 1985, 38. Bayardo appeared in a photo with President Reagan who said, "He (Bayardo) has experienced things that many of us in this country can barely imagine."

2. A new well which sadly had been needed for some years was dug in the fall of 1987 at the Guasimos Quarter of the camp in Jacaleapa. The pressure behind the U.N. action was forced upon it by one American lady, Nana Gill, who unilaterally was considering doing something such as this. There, with the help of an American-based organization called Christ in the Americas, she had considered securing a hygienic water supply for the refugees.

In the spring and summer of 1986, it was reported that as many as sixty-six children died at Teupasenti. In August of 1987, nineteen children were said to have died at Jacaleapa. It is apparent that these numbers were not documented by the officialdom involved.

Bill Stewart, an American Christian worker in the Danli area, had been appalled by the hygienic conditions in the refugee camps. He noticed that because of the water pollution, people became sick and children were dying. He counted twenty-six fresh graves of children at Jacaleapa in June and July of 1987. Before this he was aware of an epidemic of measles and the subsequent deaths of other children.

As Honduras did not sign United Nations protocol for refugees, refugees in Honduras are considered illegal aliens and controlled by the state's immigration authorities. In turn the state gave permission to the United Nations High Commissioner for Refugees (UNHCR; in Spanish, Alto Comisionado de las Naciones Unidas para Refugiados, or ACNUR) to be in charge of the refugee problem.

Though ACNUR supervises, it has given responsibility to other agencies to provide services to the refugees. These include the Catholic Relief agency, CARITAS; the International Red Cross; and Doctors Without Frontiers (MSF). These groups are supposed to be responsible for daily needs of the refugees but they only do what is barely adequate. Other humanitarian groups do come in to aid somewhat with food, clothing, and medical services.

Refugees are prohibited from developing projects in which money would have to be invested. They also are not allowed to work except in ACNUR regulated fields or in projects where earnings are returned to the local authorities.

3. "Aleksandr Solzhenitsyn," *Congressional Record* 128:1, Jan. 28, 1982, 399. The quote came from a television interview which was aired on October 26-27, 1980, on the NBC *Tomorrow* show. This interview had been done on October 12, 1980, with Congressman John Le Boutillier interviewing Solzhenitsyn by means of an English translation from the Russian language.

Frank and Tere Bendana

Grabbing for Power

1. In a letter received by the author from Dra. Lois Winner Mervyn, the Cultural Affairs Officer with the United States Information Service Office in Managua dated September 29, 1988, it was stated that even though this school kept the same administration, it was one of a number of private religious schools that was "opened to the public."

2. Cf. Humberto Belli, *Breaking Faith* (Westchester, Ill.: Crossway Books in cooperation with the Puebla Institute, 1985), 25-29.

3. "We will be new, love. The old and deprived

"We will wash away blood The vices, the tendencies,

"The putrid petite bourgeoisie."

Ibid., 13. The previous verse was taken from the work of Gioconda Belli in Bridget Aldaraca, et al., eds., *Nicaragua in Revolution: The Poets Speak* (Minneapolis: Marxist Educational Press: 1980), 275.

4. Cf. Billy James Hargis, *Forewarned*, 23—"…in reality the Communists are international outlaws"(Tulsa, Oklahoma: Christian Crusade Books: 1988), 49-55.

Having an excuse is part of the expertise of the Sandinistas, especially in fooling fellow travelers that side with them. The lie permeates everything that they do. On September 29, 1986, in Tegucigalpa, Honduras, Dr. Carlos Icaza, a spokesman for the FDN, giving an answer to the following statement and question, "Norway and Canada had recently sent aid money to Nicaragua. I don't know about Denmark," said, "I think they used to send in the past, but I don't think, right now. Basically, the problem with the Sandinistas is that of the aid they receive, they use it to buy weapons. It is more than unbelievable. It is stupid to send them any such humanitarian aid.

"Do you know that the best children's hospital in all of Central America was in Managua? This was the only thing that the Somoza family did for the country. They, of course, didn't have money. They asked the people of the country to contribute, and a very, very good hospital for children was in the process of being built. By 1979 and during the war, 90% of the physical plant of the hospital had been completed. The West German government sent all the material and equipment needed to complete the plant but the Sandinistas sold the equipment to buy weapons."

The following material is based upon information from "Marxism and Christianity in Revolutionary Central America" (Hearings chaired by Senator Jeremiah Denton before the Sub-Committee on Security and Terrorism of the Committee on the Judiciary of the United States Senate, Washington, D.C., Oct. 18-19, 1983, 164-258). (There was a special reference made to "A Document: A Revelation of a Jesuit Revolutionary," *Figaro* [from a French trans.], Sat., April 24, 1982, 32-42). Marxists have goals which are alike in purpose whether they are constituted as a nation or a guerrilla group. What Fr. [Luis Edouard] Pellecer [Faena] revealed concerning the Guerrilla Army of the Poor (EGP) in Guatemala is similar to that which has happened and is happening in other Latin American countries in that each group helps each other out. He said that the three sources for its money in Guatemala were: (1) Socialist countries, (2) theft and (3) "Humanitarian Aid."

"Humanitarian Aid" was channeled through Jesuits such as Fr. Pellecer, but then only through his personal bank account as the Jesuit Society had no legal personality. "Most of the funds (about 80%) were simply diverted to extremist organizations, and served for their living expenses or for the purchase of weapons" 238-239.

Groups that gave funds to the Jesuits were Caritas (Italy); Bread for the World, Misereor, and Adveniat, all from the Federal Republic of Germany; a Protestant group, Novib, and a Catholic group, Cebemo, from The Netherlands; Canadian Catholic Organization for Development and Peace, and a Protestant group, Christian Aid, from Canada; a Roman Catholic group, Catholic Relief Services, and the Protestant organization, the National Council of Churches, from the United States; and the World Council of Churches, 238, 247-248.

At the hearing, Fr. Pellecer further revealed that "…the Catholic Relief Service offered me the money. They said, 'We are tired of building bridges, and store houses, and schools, and supplying water. We want to really make a mark here. We went to support change and the revolutionary process.' Those were their very words" 248.

Those involved in a liberalism of our day are relentless in attempting to aid a ruthless government. Cf. Jim Ross, "Nicaragua convoy, stopped at border, back in Minnesota," *St. Paul Pioneer Press Dispatch,* Thurs., July 21, 1988, 1B.

Cf. Hargis, op. cit., 125—"…the Communist Sandinista leaders have shown what the revolution in Nicaragua really means to them…not freedom or liberty or equality for the peasants but political power and material wealth to themselves."

5. This is a Nicaraguan church movement on the part of some Catholics who stress "Christian Socialism." Claiming to be inspired by Liberation Theology which stresses the exclusivity of an outreach to the poor, this cause plays into the hands of Communist expansionism. It has its Protestant counterpart which has been working at this particular theological game for a longer time. Cf. David E. Anderson, "U.S. Church Support For Sandinistas Hit," *Washington Post,* Sat., July 14, 1984, G10.

6. Cf. Salman Rushdie, *The Jaguar Smile: A Nicaraguan Journey* (New York: Penguin Books, 1988; Viking Penguin, Inc., 1987), 63—"There was a very real possibility of a second Reformation, a second break with Rome."

Communists and American Politics

1. Consider the anger against Jose Esteban Gonzales. Cf. Klaudine Ohland and Robin Schneider (editors), "National Revolution and Indigenous Identity: The Conflict Between Sandinist[a]s and Miskito Indians on Nicaragua's Atlantic Coast," IWGIA Document No. 47, (Copenhagen: International Work Group for Indigenous Affairs, Nov. 1983—originally in German Nahua Edition, Wuppertal, 1982) from 113 in "FSLN: The Separatists are not the Atlantic Coast," *Barricada,* Feb. 28, 1981.

2. "Nicaragua to allow 10 priests to return, news show to resume" (Associated Press), *Star Tribune,* Minneapolis, Minn., Thurs., March 16, 1989, 20A.

After nearly ten years of keeping thousands of former National Guardsmen as political hostages in prison, because of the hope of ridding themselves of the Contras and for other gains, on March 17, 1989, the Sandinista government released 1,894 of these men. Daniel Ortega promised electoral and other reforms because his left-wing government was forced to do so. Cf. "Other news," *Star Tribune,* Minneapolis, Minn., Sat., March 18, 1989, 3A, and "Ex-guardsmen given pardons by Nicaragua" (Associated Press), *St. Paul Pioneer Press Dispatch,* Sat., March 18, 1989, 6A.

3. Among radical Socialists, this word means anyone with private property interests. The Sandinistas use this Marxist and Communist designation to refer to social classes between the very wealthy and the working class. "Bourgeoisie" refers to a social order dominated by the bourgeois.

Cf. Humberto Belli, *Nicaragua: Christians Under Fire* (Garden City, Mich.: The Puebla Institute, 1984), 24.

4. Cf. Belli, *Breaking Faith,* 58.

5. His complete name is Daniel Jose Ortega Saavedra.

6. A practice of these "righteous" FSLN bank robbers was to shoot tellers if it was thought that not enough money was handed over.

7. American government leaders: James C. Wright, House Democrat from Texas, and, beginning in 1987, the Speaker of the House; Bill Alexander, House Democrat from Arkansas; and Christopher J. Dodd, Democratic senator from Connecticut.

8. "Human Rights in Nicaragua," *Hearings before the Sub-Committee on Western Hemisphere Affairs of the Committee on Foreign Relations, United States Senate* (Washington, D.C., Feb. 25 and March 1, 1982).

a. Andrea I. Young, attorney, Atlanta, 29-34.—Ms. Young went to Nicaraguaon a fact finding mission with Ramsey Clark, former attorney general of the United States, on February 7-13, 1982. She appeared to be impressed by the way the Sandinistas were handling the Miskito. She said that "The country we saw was quite different from the image painted by the Reagan Administration."

A relocation camp in the Rosita area was visited by Ms. Young, who said that the children seemed relaxed and that the residents had named the camp Tasba Pry (*Tasba Pri,* which meant "Free land" in Miskito). Cf. Belli, *Breaking Faith,* 111-113, "The Miskitos: An Ethnic Tragedy."

Though a number of different ways of translating *Tasba Pry* have been given, it would not be difficult to conclude the ironic intent of the Sandinistas. According to Bernard Nietschmann, there were about four or five of these relocation camps situated in a certain zone with the same name associated with all of them. Cf. Ohland and Schneider, op.cit., 26, and Richard Harris and Carlos M. Vilas, editors, *Nicaragua: A Revolution Under Siege* (London: Zed Books, Ltd., 1985) and Gillian Brown, "Miskito Revindication: Between Revolution and Resistance," 185-186.

Bruce McColm, 34-42, said what Nicaragua did to Miskitos "...could probably be considered the single largest abuse of human rights in our hemisphere in recent memory." His organization, Freedom House, concluded that what the government is doing is to "...eradicate, spiritually, culturally, and physically the peoples of the coastal region."

Dr. William Leo Grande, 43-53, stated that the Sandinista "...government of national reconstruction with regard to rights of the person, while it is not an unblemished one, has shown a marked improvement over those of the previous regime."

Dr. Frank Bendana on pp. 53-57.

Jesse Helms reported on one person who was invited but was unable to appear. She was Sister Kenneth of the Order of St. Agnes from Fond du Lac, Wisconsin, who had worked for twenty-nine years among the Miskitos in eastern Nicaragua. It was stated that the Sandinistas had expelled her from the country for "...a rather unchristian attitude of promoting hatred for the Revolution."

9. A roll call vote on the floor of the Senate was in process.

10. The idea conveyed focuses on the point that, to rule completely, the ruthless know that there must be the willingness to eliminate all opposition who stand in the way.

Cf. Philip Zwerling and Connie Martin, *Nicaragua: A New Kind of Revolution* (Westport, Conn.: Lawrence Hill & Company, 1985), 14-15.

11. Madalyn Murray O'Hair's son, William J. Murray, gives further insights into the problems that Frank was referring to. See William J. Murray, *Nicaragua: Portrait of a Tragedy* (Toronto: Mainroads Productions Inc., 1987), 125-144.

The Freedom Fighter leader, Adolfo Calero, said on the *McNeil-Lehrer News Hour* (National Public Television, KTCA, Minneapolis-St. Paul, June 15, 1988) that the Sandinistas held 4,600 political prisoners.

12. Cf. "Nicaraguan Prisoners Denounce Harassments—They are chained inside damp places. They are confined in large numbers to unventilated cells. They are subjected to make belief executions." (trans.) *La Tribuna*, Tegucigalpa, Honduras, Wed., Nov. 5, 1986, 47.

Approximately 7,500 National Guardsmen and workers connected with the government of Somoza were initially imprisoned. Cf. Zwerling and Martin, op. cit., 144. Cf. Keesing's Contemporary Archives (London: Keesing's Publications, Longman Group Ltd., 1980), 30317-18 and (1981) 30660—"Record of World Events."

Cf. Diederich, op. cit., 252. By June 8, 1979, Somoza had swelled his National Guard numbers to over 12,000.

13. Cf. Dickey, op. cit., 67-68.

14. Cf. *Taking the Stand* (New York: Pocket Books, 1987), 550-551. "Transcripts of the Testimony of Lt. Col. Oliver L. North," from the Select Committee of the House and Senate on Secret Military Assistance to Iran and the Nicaraguan opposition, July 1987, provided by Federal News Service, Washington, D.C.

15. Cf. William F. Buckley, Jr., *Right Reason* (Garden City, N.Y.: Doubleday & Company, Inc., 1985), 300-301.

Peter Rosset and John Vandermeer (eds.), *Nicaragua: Unfinished Revolution* (New York: Grove Press Inc., 1986), 23-32; "Nicaragua's Untold Stories" by Robert Leiken from *The New Republic,* Oct. 8, 1984.

16. Cf. Dickey, op. cit., 210. In the spring of 1983, "The congressmen did not want Communists in Central America, but did not want to sign on to the tactics needed to get rid of them."

The Name, Contra

1. Cf. J. Edgar Hoover, *Masters of Deceit* (New York: Holt, Rinehart and Winston, 1958), 333-337.

2. Cf. U.S. Department of State, *Human Rights in Nicaragua Under the Sandinistas,* 18-20.

3. At the time of his expulsion from Nicaragua, Frank Bendana was a director with this organization.

"Keep Quiet"

1. Central Intelligence Agency of the United States.

2. Cf. George Szamuely, "Rushdie May Appreciate Democracy Better Now," *Wall Street Journal,* Sat., Feb. 22, 1989, A14—"...the fundamental distinctions in the world today are...between freedom and suppression of freedom. Salman Rushdie...has spent his life confusing these issues...."

3. Cf. George Russell, "Nothing Will Stop This Revolution" (reported by Timothy Loughrans, William McWhirter, and Alessandra Stanley), *Time,* Mon., Oct. 17, 1983, 37. The article makes reference to Managua as "the capital of queues."

4. A member of a traveling musical group from Nicaragua that was appealing for funds to assist the Sandinista Literacy Campaign spoke for the group when he said, "I don't think as an individual. I'm part of a community." This was reported by Carla Hall, "The Music and Message of Nicaragua," *Washington Post,* Thurs., May 8, 1980, C7.

5. Hoover, op. cit., 323.

6. In 1978, General Reynaldo Perez Vega was the Somoza National Guard's number two man who was murdered by the Sandinistas. In Managua on Sunday, February 14, 1988, Nora Astorga Gadea came to her life's end. *Wall Street Journal,* Mon., Feb. 15, 1988, A18.

Cf. Wolfgang Saxon, "Nora Astorga, Sandinista Hero And Delegate to U.N. Dies At 39," *New York Times,* Mon., Feb. 15, 1988, 20.

Cf. Art Harris, "The Sandinistas' Sister-in-Arms," *Washington Post,* Thurs., Oct. 4, 1984.

As the previous references do not explain that General Perez [Vega] was tortured, space must be taken to at least point to what Nora Astorga did as revealed by Anastasio Somoza (told to Jack Cox), *Nicaragua Betrayed* (Belmont, Mass.: Western Islands, 1980), 293: "General Vega…had been having an affair…[with Nora Astorga] for some time…On the night of the murder, General Vega went to Astorga's house and, on the allegation by Astorga that she had no liquor, he sent his driver and bodyguard away to get some…secluded in the house was a group of Sandinista cohorts of Astorga's…he was beaten into a bloody pulp…eyes gouged out…throat cut…body burned with cigarettes…genitals were cut off and stuffed in his mouth. Attending doctors estimated it took several hours for the General to die." Examine 386 and both sides of the insert before 285 which show a similar murder and torture of another victim of the Sandinistas.

See also Dickey, op. cit., 63-67.

After the Marxist takeover, Nora Astorga became the special prosecutor to seal the fate of eight thousand former members of the army of Nicaragua. Cf. Diederich, op. cit., 293.

New Indoctrination

1. Cf. Hoover, op. cit., 325-330.

2. At Medellin, Columbia, in 1968, the Bishops of Latin America decisively raised the concern for justice and social involvement within the Catholic Church.

3. Cf. Zwerling and Martin, op. cit., 14-15—Fr. Bismark Carballo said, "…the creation of the 'Popular Church,' a phenomenon of people with Marxist orientation who act as a religious mask for the Sandinistas…is not a Nicaraguan phenomenon. It was born in Chile during the time of Allende, out of a movement called 'Christians for Socialism.' Basically, their program was to try to make a breach for the entrance of Marxism into Latin America through the churches. The Popular Church…tries to justify this project as well. Marxism in Nicaragua tries to show people that Christianity doesn't have answers to their needs and that the only solution for Christians is to follow the path of Marxism. The Popular Church is a political movement with a Christian face."

4. Cf. Diederich, op. cit., 123-124. That Father Fernando Cardenal survived the possibility of being tried for treason by Somoza is credited to Donald Fraser, the Chairman of

the United States House of Representatives' House Subcommittee on Foreign Affairs. Fr. Cardenal had appeared before the committee on June 8, 1976.

Father Cardinal had been a Trappist. Cf. John A. Booth, *The End and the Beginning: The Nicaraguan Revolution* (Boulder, Colo.: Westview Press, 1985), 212.

5. Popular name for a religious group within the Roman Catholic Church known as the Society of Jesus (JS), which traces its beginning back to 1543.

6. Cf. Rushdie, op. cit., 59-62.

7. Terminology used at Medellin. See 3-E, 2.

8. Cf. Malachi Martin, *The Jesuits* (New York: The Linden Press, Simon & Schuster, Inc., 1987), 56-57—"Liberation Theology was the perfect blueprint for the Sandinistas. It incorporated the very arm of Marxist-Leninism. It presumed the classic Marxist 'struggle of the masses' to be free from all capitalist domination. And above all, the Marxist baby was at last wrapped in the very swaddling clothes of ancient Catholic terminology. Words and phrases laden with meaning for the people were co-opted and turned upside down. The historical Jesus, for example, became an armed revolutionary. The mystical Christ became all the oppressed people, collectively. Mary the Virgin became the mother of all revolutionary heroes. The Eucharist became the bread freely made by liberated workers. Hell became the Capitalist system....

"...the Sandinista undertaking was ever more brilliantly explained, refined, and dinned into the ears of seminarians, nuns, university students, and the popular mind by increasing numbers of their Jesuit, Franciscan, and Maryknoll teachers and lectures throughout the schools of Central America. The seeding time was well spent in the view of ultimate Marxisation."

9. Cf. Diederich, op. cit., 231—"...Somoza told the Voice of America's Jack Curtiss, apparently referring to his fellow Central American general-presidents also facing church opposition, 'Who do you think gets these kids [the muchachos] so worked up? The priests! Every time I go outdoors I hold on to my ribs wondering if I'll get blown up with the weapons these kids are getting now!'"

Cf. Marlise Simons, "Pope Insists Priests Quit Sandinista Posts Or He Will Not Visit," *New York Times*, Fri., Dec. 3, 1982, L-A1

10. Cf. Ronald Radosh, "Nicaragua Revisited," *New Republic*, Mon., Aug. 3, 1987, 22.

Cf. Report of the Caribbean Commission Investigative Team, "The Tragedy Of Nicaragua," (New Orleans, La.: The Caribbean Commission, 1987), 12-13.

Cf. An answer from a spokesman of the Left, Rushdie, op. cit., 64.

Frank Gone/School Duties

1. Beginning in 1979, the State Council, Nicaragua's legislative body, was supposed to represent the country in a pluralistic way. Instead, the Sandinista National Liberation Front (FSLN) took over the State Council's law-making ability by deceit and force.

Touted Literacy Program

1. Sandinista Youth "19th of July" (JS-19J or Juventud Sandinista "19 de Julio") is used by the Sandinistas in urban areas for population control and advancing its programs in connection with the CDSs, the Militias, and the Sandinista Headquarters for Workers (CST = Central Sandinista de Trabajadores), a labor confederation for urban and some farm workers.

2. Cf. Lenore Blum, "The Literary Campaign, Nicaragua Style," *Caribbean Review* (Winter 1981), 20—The Literacy Campaign funding came from the United States, Holland, and West Germany involving church groups. The author reported the cost at twenty-five million dollars. Aid came from Catholic and Protestant churches. Cuba's help was connected to the Eastern Bloc countries.

Cf. Valerie Miller, *Between Struggle and Hope: The Literacy Crusade, Westview Special Studies on Latin America and the Caribbean* (Boulder and London: Westview Press, 1985), 46: Public funds were not used; and 62: "People from Latin America, the United States, Canada and Europe came to volunteer their services as educational experts and literacy teachers. International agencies, church groups, and foreign government representatives arrived to offer financing and technical assistance."

3. Cf. Paulo Freire, *Pedagogy of the Oppressed,* 23rd printing, trans. by Myra Bergman Ramos (New York: The Continuum Corporation, 1985, from original Portuguese manuscript, 1968, copyright in 1970 by Paulo Freire), 11. In Brazil, Freire was jailed for seventy days in 1964, spent five years in Chile working for UNESCO and the Chilean Institute for Agrarian Reform, acted as a consultant at Harvard University's School of Education, and, at the time of the publication of this book, served as Special Consultant to the Office of Education of the World Council of Churches in Geneva.

Cf. Blum, op. cit., 18-21.

4. Cf. *Keesing's Contemporary Archives* (1981), 30660.

5. Cf. Christopher Dickey, "Managua Literacy Drive: Too Political?" *Washington Post,* Sat., May 24, 1980, A11. Mr. Dickey noticed "…that while 'bourgeois' and 'imperialism' are part of the basic text, 'pluralism' and 'elections' are nowhere to be seen."

Cf. Barbara Koeppel, "Nicaragua Sending All of Its Citizens to School," *Christian Science Monitor,* Thurs., Jan. 17, 1980, 5. The Literacy Campaign was under way. It was to cost twenty-one million dollars and Nicaragua was looking for donors. Already, the World Council of Churches had contributed $500,000, West Germany had sent $800,000 for notebooks and supplies, and Swedish labor unions were planning on giving 50,000 oil lamps.

6. Cf. Gordon Mott, "In Nicaragua, The Lucky Buy Plenty With Dollars," *New York Times,* Mon., Nov. 12, 1984, L-A8.

Cf. Ronald Radosh, op. cit., 20-21 "…air-conditioned shopping mall three city blocks long. Originally…open only to FSLN leaders, diplomats, and Westerners, but now any Nicaraguan who purchases an admission card for ten dollars a year can shop there…beyond the means of most people."

"Terrible Were Those Days for the Private Schools"

1. Cf. U.S. Department of State, *Human Rights in Nicaragua Under the Sandinistas,* 15.

Liberation Theology

1. Cf. Malachi Martin, op. cit., 307-317. Within these pages. it might be well to highlight 310—"Along the road in the development of Liberation Theology, a certain sleight-of-hand had taken place. 'Disinformation' is the current polite word for the process."

2. Certain political leaders in the United States, dishonestly, "turn their heads" when the discussion of land seizures is brought up. Though relatively underpopulated, Nicaragua has much land that could be farmed. Less than ten percent of available land is used. Cf. Richard A. Nuccio, *Who's Wrong Who's Right in Central America* (New York: Facts on File Publications, 1986), 45.

3. In connection with these thoughts, Tere introduced the author to a videocassette in Spanish (distributed by the Nicaraguan Information Center, c/o Dr. Alexander Bolanos, St. Charles, Missouri) which featured Fr. Luis Eduardo Pellecer, who had appeared with the National Press Club in Guatemala City, Guatemala, on September 30, 1981. Tere also translated this address that Fr. Pellecer had given to national leaders of Guatemala and foreign visitors in the country.

In attempting to build a projected new socialistic society, priests such as Fr. Pellecer began encouraging their trusting Catholic parishioners to grab for political power, even through the use of force.

To what Dr. Bolanos contributed I must add that during the my visit to Guatemala City at the end of March 1987, the Roman Catholic Curia informed me that Fr. Pellecer had married. I was informed by others that he was under protective custody.

Cf. Max Echegaray, "Central America 'Backfire': Juntas quote Pope, attack Jesuits—Jesuits' political, social involvement challenged," *National Catholic Reporter,* Kansas City,

Mo., Fri. , Feb. 8, 1980, 8—"...oligarchies and military governments accuse Jesuits of hiding machine guns under their cassocks."

Cf. Diederich, op. cit., 126—In an excerpt of a letter from Catholic Bishops in Nicaragua on the situation of human rights, Jan. 1, 1977, it was stated "There are cases in which Delegates of the Word have been taken prisoner by the Army and have been tortured, while others have disappeared."

4. Cf. Steve Askin, "Detained Jesuit Visits Washington," *National Catholic Reporter*, Fri., Dec. 31, 1982, 2.

Cf. "Fr. Pellecer's Testimony," *The Wanderer*, St. Paul, Minn., Thurs., Aug. 23, 1984, 5— "Recently, the Senate Subcommittee on Security and Terrorism released testimony disclosed at its hearings last October on 'Marxism and Christianity in Revolutionary Central America.' The printed testimony was delayed because Sen. Patrick Leahy (D. Vt.) was of the opinion that testimony of another witness had not been sufficiently corroborated regarding involvement of some religious people in guerrilla activity."

In spite of Sen. Leahy's later put-down, "The former priest testified under oath '...when I was working as a Jesuit priest, under the orders of my superiors, we utilized Marxist-Leninist ideology...'

"The former priest continued: '...the theology of liberation is used to delegitimize the capitalist system, and to give legitimacy to the socialist system....

"'...the theology of liberation can be better stated as the theology of revolution.'"

Concerns Including the Pope's Visit

1. Cf. Zwerling and Martin, op. cit., 18—Fr. Carballo said that the church had "...permitted masses to be held wherever the soldiers had fallen and died...But the problem was that many times these masses in the streets became political acts of the government. Our principle now is that we celebrate such masses only in the church for whoever has died."

2. For a description of the Pope's visit, see Malachi Martin, op. cit., 114-120.

To assess a biased accounting of the Pope's visit, cf. William R. Callahan and Dolores C. Pomerleau, "'Irresponsible' Words Polarize Nicaragua," *National Catholic Reporter*, Wed., March 25, 1983.

"Live in a Country of Fear and Silence"

1. In Honduras in 1987, a Jehovah's Witness foreign missionary told the author that all foreign Jehovah's Witness missionaries in Nicaragua had been expelled in 1982. At that time, because one of them was spotted by news media as he was leaving the country at the airport in Managua, Sandinista officials allowed him to remain a few months longer.

Also in 1987 in Honduras, a leader representing the Mormon Church in Honduras told the author that Mormons would not send any of their missionaries into Nicaragua. This person also said that of the half dozen pieces of property which had been seized from them, one or two had not been returned.

Cf. "Sects Under Attack in Nicaragua," *New York Times,* Thurs., Aug. 12, 1988, L-A3.

Cf. Belli, *Nicaragua: Christians Under Fire,* 48—After May in 1982, churches belonging to "…the Moravians, Adventists, Mormons, and Jehovah's Witnesses were confiscated in rapid succession by the authorities."

2. On September 12, 1987, Fr. Bismark Carballo Madrigal returned to Nicaragua as part of a political strategy being worked on by the Sandinista government in conjunction with a peace plan negotiated by five other Central American nations. See *Facts on File,* Fri., Sept. 25, 1987, 687-F1 and D3—"Central America."

"Enormous Communciation, Little True Information"

1. Cf. Bernard Weintraub, "Reagan Urges Arms Aid for Nicaraguan Rebels," *New York Times,* Sun., Dec. 15, 1985, L-A1.

2. Cf. Hargis, op. cit., 94—"Communism cannot be established without force and bloodshed and it cannot be maintained in power without coercive measures and enforced servitude."

3. Cf. Russell Stendal, *Rescue the Captors* (Burnsville, Minn.: Ransom Press International, 1984), 3rd ed., 188.

Daisy Montiel Rodriguez
"Beautiful Country…Being Spoiled"

1. Cf. U.S. Department of State, *Human Rights in Nicaragua Under the Sandinistas* (Permanent Commission on Human Rights of Nicaragua, Managua, Sept. 11, 1985), 218-220—"Report on the Prison Situation—Nicaragua 1985." El Chipote, a maximum security institution controlled by the secret police, is one of nine State Security prisons that function outside the laws of Nicaragua. Carcel Modelo and Zona Franca are both part of the National Penitentiary system. Zona Franca has special cells known as "Extermination cells."

2. Cf. Belli, *Breaking Faith,* 248—This person was "…a young Liberal Party dissident" who in 1956 assassinated General Anastasio Somoza Garcia, the President of Nicaragua.

3. Op. cit. The September 1988 letter addressed to the author from the United Information Service in Managua stated that the Annunciation School, Pureza de Maria, and Teresian Academy were also "opened to the public" but remained girls' schools.

Manuel Jiron

"Mystique...Charisma...Charm"

1. Cf. Walter Goodman, *The Committee* (New York: Farrar, Straus and Giroux, 1986), 433. J. Edgar Hoover is quoted: "The Communist success in San Francisco in May 1960 proves it can happen here [meaning within the United States]."

2. These groups and individuals represented a political direction for a more democratic Nicaragua. They were not as organized, supplied, nor armed as the Sandinista Party had been with its close connection to Cuba, Russia, and the other left-wing forces of the world, including liberals of all shapes and sizes.

3. Cf. Zwerling and Martin, op. cit., 16—Speaking of Nicaragua and Sandinista leadership, Fr. Carballo said, "...now there is no liberty here."

4. This was the newspaper owned by the Somoza family and called *Novidades*. The Sandinistas expropriated it in 1979 for FSLN Party use and named it *Barricada*.

5. Cf. "La Prensa Is Crusading Critic of Nicaragua Regime," *Star Tribune,* Minneapolis, Minn., Sun., March 13, 1988, 23A. Because of the peace accords of 1987, *La Prensa* was allowed to print again with the first issue published on October 1, 1987.

6. Cf. Susan Bennett, "Bush changes course with Contras," *St. Paul Pioneer Press Dispatch,* Sat., March 25, 1989, 3A—"The compromise on U.S Central American policy was more noteworthy for its unity than its innovation...plan calls for the Contras to receive U.S. money for food, housing, medical supplies and clothing, just as Reagan proposed once he realized that Congress would not approve military aid."

"Contras call for new aid after talks collapse," *Star Tribune,* Minneapolis, Minn., Sat., June 11, 1988, 3A.

Cf. Nina M. Serafino, *Contra Aid: 1981-March 1987—Summary and Chronology of Major Congressional Action on Key Legislation Concerning U.S. Aid to the Anti-Sandinista Guerrillas* (Washington, D.C.: Congressional Research Service, The Library of Congress, Tues., July 21, 1987.)

Cf. *Taking The Stand,* 605. Commenting on the Boland Amendments, which were also in effect from October 1, 1984, to October 18, 1986, and which prohibited the provision of military assistance to the Freedom Fighters, Representative Henry Hyde of Illinois revealed how the Democrats of the House of Representatives forced these amendments into a major, national budget bill which had to be signed by President Ronald Reagan.

But on the next to the last week of December of 1987, President Reagan turned a same trick on the Democrats when he was successful in obtaining sorely needed Freedom Fighters funds because the Democrats were interested in going home for the Christmas and New Years holidays.

Cf. "Iran-Contra Affair," *Report of the Combined Select House Committee to Investigate Covert Arms Transactions with Iran and Senate Committee on Secret Military Assistance to Iran and the Nicaraguan Opposition* (Section II, "The Minority Report," 439-633, Washington, D.C., 1987).

Cf. "Iran-Contra Investigation" (*Select Committee On Secret Military Assistance to Iran and the Nicaraguan Opposition and the House Select Committee to Investigate Covert Arms Transactions With Iran—Testimony of Richard V. Secord, May 5 through May 8, 1987—Washington, D.C., 1988*). On page 35 in his opening statement concerning the Iran-Contra Investigation, Michael DeWine, a Representative in Congress from Ohio, threw into focus what Congress had done for the Freedom Fighters. "In 1969 and 1970, we gave to the Sandinistas. In 1981 and 1982, we gave to the Contras. In 1983 and 1984, we gave a little to the Contras, but only for nonmilitary activities.

"In 1985, we gave no aid to the Contras. In 1986, we gave some humanitarian aid, some intelligence, and some communication equipment.

"Now, in 1987, we are giving aid again. All the while, the Soviets are giving uninterrupted to the Sandinistas, to the tune of hundreds of millions of dollars."

7. This thought persists with the friends of the United States who are being turned away from their fight for freedom. Cf. Michael Wines and Doyle McManus, "Contra-White House meeting reflected fading hopes of Victory," *Star Tribune,* Minneapolis, Minn., Fri., March 25, 1988, A1.

8. Murdered in 1978, he became the national martyr around whom was ignited the spark for the insurrection that defeated Somoza, who was blamed for the killing. Chamorro's death wasmost likely the work of the Sandinistas.

8. Cf. Belli, Nicaragua—Christians Under Fire, 70-71—Photographs describing Manuel Jiron with a head wound that required fourteen stitches detailed the account of how he was assaulted while in his car with his wife and four of his children, aged three to nine years. Passers-by thwarted the attempt. The photos and article were reprinted from *La Prensa,* Mon., Jan. 18, 1982.

9. Manuel Jiron, (editor), *Quien es Quien en Nicaragua* (San Jose, Costa Rica: Editoral Radio Amor, 1986).\

Takeover Montage

1. Cf. Hargis, op. cit., 124—"The U.N. supports terrorism, exercises a double standard for Communism and against anti-Communism, and fights rather consistently against free enterprise."

2. Known by its acronym, OAS, this is a longtime, established organization working on behalf of the North and South American continents.

3. A commission which conducted its first meeting on the Panamanian island of Contadora consists of the following nations: Colombia, Mexico, Panama, and Venezuela.

4. In 1988, the total number of Freedom Fighters at war against the Sandinista government of Nicaragua was somewhere in the neighborhood of 22,000.

5. At the end of 1987, the author received a report from someone considered very reliable who had hitchhiked in and out of Nicaragua. As he was considered an Internationalist, this hiker was not checked for identification except at border crossings. During bus journeys, everyone else was searched except those who appeared to be foreigners. The hitchhiker surmised that the average Nicaraguan citizen knows that he or she is in a police state and does not like nor trust those who have come to serve the Sandinistas who have inflicted great turmoil upon the family and the social order.

6. Cf. Jiron, op. cit., 305-307—Edgard D. Parrales had been involved with the Christian Brothers and was ordained as a priest. He even served as the chaplain to the mother of Anastasio Somoza Debayle. From 1969 and on he became associated with the Sandinista guerrilla movement and when it came to power, he was appointed to serve in Social Welfare. Diverting funds from the United Nations assistance for refugees, he channeled aid to Salvadoran guerrillas. A man with affection for wine and women, Parrales was an important factor in sending Nicaraguan youth to be indoctrinated in Communist Cuba. The 1981 Nicaraguan representative to the OAS, now with other work in Nicaragua, he sends $2,000 a month to a relative in the United States.

Cf. Philip Taubman, "U.S. Says It Halted Talks With Nicaragua—Four Nicaraguan Priests Suspended," *New York Times,* Sat., Jan. 19, 1985, L-A4.

Cf. "Vatican Criticizes Office-Holding Nicaraguan Priests," *The Wanderer,* St. Paul, Minn., Thurs., Aug. 23, 1984, 1—In 1985 Parrales became the Minister of Social Welfare.

7. In the fall of 1987 and at the time of the first Freedom Fighter-Sandinista cease fire talks, hundreds of prisoners were to have been released from Sandinista prisons. Associated with this time was the reopening of *La Prensa* and Catholic Radio. Although Fr. Carballo returned to Nicaragua, Bishop Vega refused to do so until civil rights were restored in the country.

On July 11, 1988, *La Prensa* for the second time that year was closed by the government, along with Catholic Radio—Cf. "Nicaragua expels U.S. envoy, cites 'state terrorism'," *Star Tribune,* Minneapolis, Minn., Tues., July 12, 1988, 1A.

"In several different peace negotiations the Sandinistas agreed to discuss an amnesty for the former Guard members and for captured rebel guerrillas. Groups of prisoners were released in limited amnesties…Plans for release were dropped when cease-fire talks broke down last summer. But they were revived last month at a regional summit meeting in Tesoro

Beach, El Salvador."—Mark A. Uhlig, "Somoza's Soldiers Rejoining a Society Divided on Pardon," *New York Times,* Fri., March 17, 1989, 4Y.

8. Read Douglas W. Payne's research, "The Democratic Mask—The Consolidation of the Sandinista Revolution," from *Perspectives On Freedom* 3, New York: Freedom House (1951), 20, 24—In June of 1979 before the fall of Somoza, an agreement with the Sandinistas was made at Puntarenas, Costa Rica, by Nicaraguan political leaders as to how Nicaraguan was to be governed. The Sandinistas did not keep this agreement.

9. The FSLN National Directorate was made up of various factions within the Sandinista leadership which had no problems with ideology. It only had to decide the best method of gaining and maintaining governmental power which, today, in Nicaragua it controls dictatorially.

Salvador Montenegro

"Neither a Dictator Nor a Democrat"

1. The histories of the Liberal and Conservative Parties trace back to the time of Nicaraguan independence from Spain in 1823. Each party was family-centered, with the Conservatives (Los Conservativos) tending to be more traditional, pro-church, and landowner oriented, with their center in Granada. The Liberals' (Los Liberales) traditional center was Leon. Though still Catholic, they wanted to abolish church privileges and take over its wealth. This brought the Liberal Party more power with their desire to follow the more dramatic patterns of change mirrored in Western countries.

These parties never achieved complete success for their ideas and programs, which mainly served to enrich their own political personalities. However, progress was slowly being accomplished in Nicaragua.

2. Cf. Philip Zwerling and Connie Martin, op. cit., 206-213.

3. Anastasio Somoza Portocarrero, the son of Anastasio Somoza Debayle.
    Cf. Diederich, op. cit., 140-141, 144.

4. Cf. Belden Bell, ed., *Nicaragua: An Ally Under Siege,* "Nicaragua's Economy" by William Schneider, Jr., (Washington, D.C.: Council On American Affairs, 1978), 104-112.

Cause of Somoza's Fall

1. a. Cf. "Ortega says contra war is over, offers peace effort" (from Washington Post), *Star Tribune,* Minneapolis, Minn., Thurs., Feb. 2, 1989, 11A. Former U.S. President Jimmy Carter, who visited with Ortega in Venezuela, attempted to keep his fingers in the turmoil of Central America.

Cf. "Ortega gives U.N. plan to repatriate contra rebels" (from news services), *Star Tribune,* Minneapolis, Minn., Wed., April 19, 1989, 16A—"…Ortega's plan…calls for creating an international commission to disarm the contras and for releasing 2,000 rebels from Nicaraguan jails.

"In related developments yesterday: Contra leaders in Miami accused the Nicaraguan government of unleashing a preelection campaign of repression and murder, and a human-rights group offered some unprecedented confirmation.

"Contra directors…accused the Sandinistas military of killing 40 to 50 civilians over the past two months in northern Nicaraguan provinces, where contra support has been the strongest, including 13 in the town of Apantillo.

"For the first time, the human-rights group Americas Watch agreed that the Sandinistas were killing suspected rebel sympathizers in the countryside. 'We cannot dismiss them as isolated incidents anymore,' said Americas Watch spokesman Juan Mendez in Washington."

2. Somoza (as told to Jack Cox), op. cit., fourth insert photo from 268.

3. Cf. Diederich, op. cit., 115—"…a $46 million trade surplus in 1976…coffee sales in 1974 tallied $46 million…doubled in 1976…more than 150 in 1977…. Inflation was down to 3 percent in 1976 from a high of 17 percent in 1974 and that year the country's gross national product grew by 8 percent."

4. Colonel Enrique Bermudez Varela

Pastor Ricardo Duarte
Life's Prelude

1. At this time the name of the airport was Las Mercedes.

Mission Price Increase

1. Gringo—White North American from the United States.

2. Within the next eighteen days, Campanerio was killed in an ambush by Contra forces who knew whom they were setting a trap for. Flaco met his death by an ambush at a much later date.

"People Must Know"

1. *Guayaba* is Spanish for guava. It has a green, bumpy, and ova-shaped exterior and is used as a fruit drink and very tasty as a jam or jelly.

2. Subtle are those who labor with the Left. Cf. "World of Religion," *Washington Post,* Sat., Oct. 20, 1984, C10. The National Council of Churches fact-finding team said that there was no evidence of a policy of religious persecution by the government of Nicaragua.

Diego Lacayo Oyanguren
Leaders In Nicaragua

1. Cf. Diederich, op. cit., 154—"In his book, *Our Neighbor Nicaragua,* published in New York in 1929, Floyd Cramer, describing the Conservatives of Granada, wrote 'The families of the Chamorros, Cadros, Lacayos always have been looked upon as royal families.'"

2. The Sandinistas violated Papal agreement by having Ernesto meet the Pope upon his arrival at the airport in Managua during the 1983 Nicaraguan Papal visit. Cf. Shirley Christian, *Nicaragua: Revolution in the Family,* 268.

3. Ibid., 332.

"A Place of Danger"

1. Instituto Pedagogico La Salle de Managua.

2. Central American University Jose Simeon Canas is a Jesuit institution.

3. For another view of what took place, cf. Christian, op. cit., 35, 36-37, 51, 341-344 (a Sandinista explanation with a rebuke of this explanation by Violeta Chamoro).

4. Cf. Diederich, op. cit., 116, 135-139.

5. Cf. ibid., 279—"It was true that most of the press was hostile to Somoza." This did not stem only from the careless National Guard killing of ABC newsman, Bill Stewart—ibid., 269-270.

6. Cf. ibid., 117—"...Guerrillas, mostly from middle-class urban families, were successful recruiting growing numbers of peasants to their cause."

7. Bernard Diederich minimized the Sandinista role in its manipulation of young Nicaraguans—Cf. ibid., 189-204. Notable also is how lightly Diederich explains the killing but not the torture of General Perez Vega—ibid., 218. A comparison could be made of how American news media emphasized, even into 1988, the role of "drug kings." Very rarely mentioned were the strategic actions that the Left was carrying out in this tragedy.

8. Cf. Richard Bourdreau, "Economic Woes Nicaragua's Top Problem," *Star Tribune,* Minneapolis, Minn., Fri., Nov. 27, 1987, A24. From *Los Angeles Times* date line, Managua, Nicaragua—"...Cordoba's rate of exchange with the dollar has plunged from 70-1 in 1979

to 3,700-1 at the start of this year to well past 13,000. The largest bill, a 5,000 cordoba note, is worth less than 35 U.S. cents."

In December of 1987, the rate had shifted to around 17,000 cordobas per dollar, with the Black Market rate even going to 21,000.

Cf. "Ortega announces austerity plan for Nicaragua" (Associated Press), *Star Tribune,* Minneapolis, Minn., Tues., Jan. 31, 1989, 1A—"...inflation...reached 20,000 percent last year...."

Book II—Citizens of Eastern Nicaragua
Joralia Wallace
"Proud Community...Subjugated"

1. A mixed race living in eastern and northeastern Nicaragua and eastern Honduras generally known as the Mosquitia, Miskitos think of their region as one small country and do not recognize the national borders. Because most of them live south of the Coco River, the Indians are accustomed to consider it as Nicaraguan. In 1960, the World Court created a Nicaraguan-Honduran international boundary along the river. Miskitos feel that they were not consulted in this dismembering of their nation.

2. See Ida Dox, *Melloni's Illustrated Medical Dictionary* (2nd ed., Baltimore: Williams and Wilkins, 1985), 372. A shortened definition of phocomelia can be stated as "Gross underdevelopment of extremities, particularly, the upper limbs...."

3. Brother James A. Miller, FSC (Brothers of the Christian Schools), an American from Stevens Point, Wisconsin, was killed at the age of thirty-seven at the De La Salle Indian House in Huehuetenango, Guatemala. The Guatemalan army had been snatching underaged boys from the Indian school and forcing them into the army. Brother Miller had just given the army men his direct feeling on the matter, and this could easily have been the reason why he was killed. But in a country where Communists are available to stir up trouble, who knows who might have been the perpetrators.

4. Former FSLN fighters, now civic leaders, dressed in uniforms and wore side arms.

5. According to Bernard Nietschmann from the University of California at Berkeley, there were 4,000 Chinese in Nicaragua. Threatened by the Sandinistas before Somoza fell, nearly all had left by July 22, 1979. These merchants were good in their trade and would customarily undersell everybody else. The Sandinistas used the Chinese as a wedge in political power plays. The Chinese had homes and property which could be confiscated by the new government officials. Professor Nietschmann suggested that someone should make a study of these Nicaraguans.

No One to Relate Stories to

1. Cf. Belli, *Breaking Faith,* 115.

2. Approximately 50,000 Miskito, Sumo, and Rama Indians were displaced by the Sandinistas and some one hundred villages were destroyed. Cf. U.S. Department of State, *Human Rights in Nicaragua Under the Sandinistas,* 190-193—"Indian Nations and the Nicaraguan State," a document by Bernard Nietschmann.

Cf. Leiken and Rubin, op. cit., 271-273—"Bernard Nietschmann: Statement to the OAS—October 1983."

Cf. Rushdie, op. cit., 76—"'We made many mistakes,'" and 130-131—"The autonomy project was FSLN's way of recognizing that they had made a series of disastrous alienating mistakes on the Atlantic coast. Inexperienced, over-zealous young political cadres had arrived among the Creoles and the Indians and created a good deal of bad feeling, for instance by making all manner of promises, of new hospitals, schools, and so forth, promises that the government quickly discovered it couldn't deliver, because of the war, the scarcities and the inaccessibility of the region."

3. The Moravian Church is a Protestant group first organized in Herrenhut, Saxony, in 1722 on the estates of the religious reformer, Count Nikolaus Zinzendorf, as a reconstitution of the fifteenth-century Bohemian Brethren. Though they have no specific creed, they do agree in substance with the Nicene Creed, the Westminster and Augsburg Confessions, and the Thirty-nine Articles. The Bible is the only guide in faith and conduct. Infant baptism is practiced, but full church membership requires a voluntary profession of faith. There is a special stress upon fellowship and missionary work. Its music is world renowned.

During the Hearings before the Subcommittee on Security and Terrorism of the Committee on the Judiciary of the United State Senate (Washington, D.C., Dec. 18 and 19, 1987) 129, Wycliffe Diego, an ordained Miskito Moravian Pastor and Freedom Fighter, said that seventy percent of the population on the East Coast of Nicaragua were Moravians. He said that the Miskitos did not like Sandino, who in the 1930s killed some Moravian pastors and burned books.

Miskito Indian Politics

1. ALPROMISO means Alliance for Progress of the Miskitos and Sumos. Founded in 1973 its goals were as follows: the restoration of control over communal lands, teaching of both Miskito and Spanish, representation in Managua, and creation of jobs. Indian leaders were beginning to have some influence with the Somoza government just before the Sandinista takeover.

In the aftermath of the mayhem they produced on the East Coast, the Department of Zelaya, in 1987, the Sandinistas divided it into two sections: the North Atlantic Autonomous Region (RAAN) and the South Atlantic Autonomous Region (RAAS).

2. After the words, "Miskito, Sumo, Rama, Sandinista," the word *aslatakanka* was added, which can be translated "united with" or "united and happening with," implying association with the Sandinistas. Cf. Ohland and Schneider, op. cit., 40—from "Misurasata: 'Together We Build A Just Society!'" in *Barricada*, Tues., Nov. 27, 1979).

For the Miskitos this would have had Biblical overtones. The Communists were not missing anything. Ortega's source could have been one of the verses in Ezekiel such as 11:19a—"And I will give them one heart, and I will put a new spirit within you."

3. With prompting from the Sandinistas, the political stage was now being set for MIS-URASATA, which had a much wider base than ALPROMISO and included the organizing of more groups such as the gold miners, women, mothers, etc.

The Miskito leadership was organized under the MISURASATA name on November 11, 1979. See Ohland and Schneider, op cit., 9.

4. At Rus Rus, Honduras, in June 1987, Steadman Fagoth Muller was chosen again as one of the leaders among East Coast Freedom Fighters. Previous to this meeting at Rus Rus, he had been leading a few members that had come out from the organization, MISURA, the largest Miskito exile organization (signifying the Miskito, Sumo, and Rama Indian tribal groupings) which he originally had helped to create.

5. There were 2,449 Miskitos returned to Nicaragua in the period from January to October 1987 according to the United Nations reports. In contrast only fifty-five Ladinos were "repatriated."

6. Cf. Jack Epstein and J.H. Evans, "Indians, Sandinistas vie for control in Nicaragua," *National Catholic Reporter*, Mon., Oct. 22, 1982, 26—In Puerto Cabezas, a Miskito Indian said to these writers, "The Sandinistas don't trust the coast people, and the coast people don't trust them."

Edwin Muller

Accounts of Atrocities

1. Cf. Lightly brushing upon the terrible truth, Stephen Kinzer fashioned a subdued report from a concentration camp three and one half years later. Read his article, "The Way Home Is Hard For Indians of Nicaragua," *New York Times*, Thurs., Aug. 22, 1985, L-A2.

"Sense Of Survival…Keenly Sharpened"

1. Because of this political climate, Edwin Muller was unable to be with his mother before she died in December 1986.

2. Cf. John Borrell, "Nicaragua At War With Itself," *Time*, Mon., Nov. 16, 1987, 41—Concerning a young man killed in action against U.S.-backed Contras, "…no honor guard and no red-and-black flag draped over the coffin…

    "As the coffin was lowered into the earth, the protest grew more voluble. 'You sons of bitches are killing us like dogs!' yelled a tear-stained pallbearer, pointing his finger at an official of the local Sandinista defense committee. 'Just leave us alone.'"

3. The Mexican-born member of the Sandinista National Directorate is Victor Tirado Lopez.

"Truksulu"

"Man Tries One Plan, But God Has Another"

1. In contrast to this number, the Sandinista estimation of the East Coast population count was very, very low, especially for the Miskitos and the Creoles, as it apparently suited the FSLN's subjugation desire for this area as recorded in 1981 by their CIDCA (Investigation & Documentation Centre for the Atlantic Coast). In editing for the 2000 publication of this book, the author thought it best to note that this impression was founded upon the book *Nicaragua—Self-Determination & Survival* by Hazel Smith, Pluto Press, 1993. Ms. Smith got her facts from the Catholic Institute of International Relations (CIIR), "Right To Survive: Human Rights in Nicaragua," 103 (London, 1987), which had picked up their facts from the CIDCA, as previously cited.

    According to the author's January 28, 2000, telephone conversation with Armstrong Wiggins at the Indian Law Resource Center, Washington, D.C., an early standard estimate of the population was 215,000. Wiggins said that Indian leaders have been reluctant to give any factual numerical amount, preferring to keep the numbers unkown.

2. Cf. Ohland and Schneider, op. cit., 38 (*Barricada*, Nov. 27, 1979). The meetings were conducted November 8-11, 1979.

3. Lyster Athders, a Miskito leader from Saklin, was arrested in the third week of September of 1979, taken to Puerto Cabezas, and murdered in October.

    Cf. Belli, *Breaking Faith,* 108.

4. Cf. Report of the Caribbean Commission Investigative Team, 5-6. By 1979, Somoza had incurred a debt of $1.5 billion with exports of $650 million. At the time of the Caribbean Commission's report, the Sandinista foreign debt was estimated at eight to nine billion dollars, with exports of barely $230 million.

Awareness of Something

1. Cf. Belli, op. cit., 108. Roger Suarez was the leader of the Puerto Cabezas workers union.

2. Cf. Beverly Treumann, "Chronicle of a Crusade (1)—Nicaragua's Second Revolution," *Christianity and Crises,* Mon., Nov. 2, 1981, 298—"The first five-month stage of the Literacy Crusade in Spanish ended on August 23, 1980. The crusade in Miskito, Sumo and English…began on the Atlantic coast in October and ended in late March 1981."

Provocation in Prinzapolka

1. KISAN had been the largest of the Indian-organized opposition groups against the Sandinistas. The name means United Indigenous Peoples of Eastern Nicaragua. Cf. U.S. Department of State, *Dispossessed—The Miskito Indians in Sandinista Nicaragua* (Washington, D.C., June 1986), 6.

Led by Wycliffe Diego, an ordained Moravian pastor, KISAN had been preceded by the organizational name, FAUCAN, which meant Atlantic Coast United Armed Force of Nicaragua. FAUCAN had been promoted by the Honduran Army and the United States, but it did not succeed because the Miskitos were not behind the idea.

When Miskitos fled Nicaragua after the jailing of the MISURASATA leaders, the new organization that was formed in exile emerged as MISURA and was led by Steadman Fagoth. MISURA came from taking the last four letters out of MISURASATA. Brooklyn Rivera later led Freedom Fighters in the Southeast of Nicaragua and continued using the title MISURASATA. With the downfall of Steadman Fagoth, KISAN came into existence.

Cf. Douglas W. Payne, "The Democratic Mask…," op. cit., 100.

2. Cf. Diederich, op. cit., 311—"For forty-six years a Somoza had ruled Nicaragua—not always as president, but always a chief of the National Guard from the day in January 1933 it had been bequeathed to Nicaragua by the United States Marines."

Cf. Craig L. Dozier, *Nicaragua's Mosquito Shore: The Years of British and American Presence* (University of Alabama: The University of Alabama Press, 1985), 231-232.

3. Cf. Ohland and Schneider, op. cit.—Julio's last name was Lopez, according to the *Barricada* article, "FSLN: The Separatists are not the Atlantic Coast."

4. Cf. "8 Killed In Nicaragua In Separatist Revolt," *Washington Post,* Tues., Feb. 24, 1981, A8. This Reuters news dispatch from Managua was delivered at a news conference granted by a leading Sandinista, Sergio Ramirez, who was later to become the country's vice president. He said that four soldiers and four rebels were killed in a clash on February 23 in Prinzapolka. He went on to claim that the four rebels were members of MISURASATA, a group comprised of indigenous Indians seeking a breakaway from Nicaragua of the Caribbean coastal areas.

Cf. an accounting of the fomentation in Prinzapolka by Christian, op. cit., 302-303.

Cf. the statements by Brooklyn Rivera in Ohland and Schneider, op. cit., "Brooklyn Rivera (MISURASATA): 'We are part of this Revolution'"—interview by Michael Rediske in Managua, April 1, 1981, 124-125.

Bows and Arrows

1. Cf. Dozier, op. cit., 233-234.

Cf. Ohland and Schneider, op. cit., 115-116, from "Government of National Reconstruction JGRN: Strong Denial of *La Prensa*'s Allegations" (*Barricada*, Sat., Feb. 28, 1981)—It is informative to note how the Sandinistas attempted to defuse and to gain from the incident. An extra insight should be added in that the Sandinistas reported that the head of Julio Lopez had been severed. But on January 28, 2000, "Truksulu," whose name is Enario Danny and is now living in the United States, said this was untrue.

2. Following the earthquake in 1972, CEPAD (Comite Evangelico pro Ayuda al Desarrollo, Evangelical Committee for Development Assistance) began as an umbrella organization for a number of Nicaraguan Protestant churches. Though its officers had worked with Somoza, they actively sided with the actions and positions taken by the Sandinista government in whatever its Communist propaganda stress might have called for. (Further insights on this subject can be read in the Report of the Caribbean Commission Investigation Team, op. cit.).

The Rev. Norman Bent worked for CEPAD in its Puerto Cabezas office. After the Sandinista takeover, he went to Managua as a leader in the Moravian Church and cleverly defended the Sandinista government in its needs. Cf. Zwerling and Martin, op. cit., 169-179.

Eunice Hooker Sang

"Prefer the Times of Somoza"

1. *Piricuacos* is the Spanish word for "rabid dogs," the name Nicaraguans give to their Sandinista rulers and those who collaborate with them.

2. Puerto Cabezas.

3. Colonel Julio Cesar Fonseca Talavera was killed by the Sandinistas in November of 1979.

4. Cf. Dozier, op. cit., 232—Miskito "...support of the regime [Somoza] was expressed by the disproportionate number of Mosquito men in the National Guard."

5. Cf. Diederich, op. cit., 129-130.

"He Is A 'Jifilifi'!"

1. Alvin Guthrie Rivers was considered as the most prominent independent labor leader in opposition to the Sandinistas.

"Stupid Ones! They Are Going to Kill You!"

1. Cf. Rushdie, op. cit., 146, 153—This author's attack upon the widow of Pedro Joaquin Chamorro included revealing her custom of wearing and displaying jewelry.

2. Cf. U.S. Department of State, *Human Rights in Nicaragua Under the Sandinistas,* 61. The Sandinistas would have liked to have had the sixty-three-year-old Bishop Salvador Schlaefer killed at the time. The whole international community realized this.

Cf. "Nicaragua: Rebels Killed U.S.-born Bishop," *Star Tribune,* Minneapolis, Minn., Thurs., Dec. 22, 1983, A14. Though a very difficult task for villagers to accomplish their flight, they choose to do it. The Bishop was accompanied by Fr. Wendelin Schafer, who was sixty-four.

In a special report in the *New York Times,* "Priest Assesses Nicaraguan Tribes' Lot," Tues., Jan. 3, 1984, A15, Fr. Schafer, who had spent thirty-six years in Nicaragua, charged that the Nicaraguan government's efforts to impose their type of government upon the Miskito, Suma, and Rama Indians caused them to become rebels.

"So Keep Your Mouth Shut"

1. This reference might be made toward any Honduran. The intent however was directed toward Miskito Indians who were indigenous citizens of Honduras who lived in this sizable, largely uninhabited, and very undeveloped state or department of Honduras known as Gracias a Dios.

2. a. John Baldwin, a humanitarian from Los Angeles, California, who manages an organization called Mercy Flight and a friend of Miskito Indians in eastern Honduras from both Honduras and Nicaragua, said, "If you give a Miskito an ax and a tree, one of the two has to go." He explained that the methods of slashing and burning have always been the traditional way of life for the small, simple farming operations of Central America. "Honduran officials," he added, "have shown great patience toward the influx of the many refugees who have come into the country."

With recent seasons of Central American dry spells, conflagrations put more pressure upon the already overburdened feelings of the displaced Miskito refugees.

3. Father Hugh Heinzen, OFM CAP (Order of Franciscans Minor, Capuchins).

4. These three sisters belong to the Sisters of Charity from Spain. In Puerto Lempira they conduct a small clinic.

Carlos Muller Schrader

"Bad Sandinista Character Was Not Seen"

1. Cf. Edmund W. and Julia Robb, *The Betrayal of the Church* (Westchester, Ill.: Crossway Books, 1986), 138—"By 1985 the regime had herded approximately eighteen thousand Indians into thirteen concentration camps, only six of which they acknowledged."

2. Cf. Belli, *Nicaragua: Christians Under Fire*, 78—"Major relocations of people have continued to occur. In December 1982 the Sandinistas forcibly relocated another contingent of approximately 10,000 Miskitos who lived in the Jinotega province. During this process an overcrowded, Soviet-made helicopter crashed, killing about 50 Miskito children, mostly teenagers. (Strangely enough, all four members of the crew escaped unharmed.)"

3. Eden Pastora became leader of a group called Democratic Revolutionary Alliance (ARDE) which was a coalition of four organizations. He demanded the leadership of all Freedom Fighter organizations and was always considered with suspicion from the United States. His support base collapsed and he ceased fighting in 1986. Fighters from within this group then joined the Nicaraguan Resistance.

4. Cf. Jeff Gerth, "On The Trail Of Latin Mystery, C.I.A. Footprints," *New York Times,* Thurs., Oct. 6, 1983, A1, 12—Agustin M. Romain was the name of the pilot.

    The aircraft was a piston-driven Cessna 404—a 1981 model. Ordinarily, it held eight to ten passengers in an unpressurized cabin and could cruise at a maximum speed of 250 mph.

5. The United States senators, Democrat Gary Hart from Colorado and Maine's Republican William S. Cohen, happened to be in the Central American area at the time. Senator Cohen's reaction was quoted in the *Star Tribune,* Minneapolis, Minn., Fri., Sept. 9, 1983, 13A. In a call to his office in the States, he said the bombing was "amateurish."

    What did he expect in a civil war where friends of the United States had to make use of what they had? To his credit, Senator Cohen voted consistently for aid to the Freedom Fighters.

Father Hugh Heinzen

"Forced to Attend Lectures"

1. One of three fraternities of men within the Franciscan Order, the Capuchins are known as the Friars Minor, the Little Brothers. The group takes its name from the cowl or hood

which is part of the traditional habit. There are approximately 15,000 Capuchin priests serving in various parts of the world.

2. In a letter written to the author from Puerto Lempira, Honduras, dated February 27, 1988, Father Heinzen explained, "There were three of the Sisters of St. Agnus from Fond du Lac, Wisconsin [Sisters Kenneth, Peter, and Rose Kowalski], and two of us Capuchin (Franciscan) Priests [including Father Joseph N. Wold] that were expelled on the 12th of January 1982.... They [Sandinistas] used the excuse that we had not renewed our resident papers for 1982. Of course, our papers were in the office [of the authorities] but they hadn't processed them."

Following the Regional Peace Plan signing in Guatemala by the presidents of five Central American countries on August 7, 1987, Sisters Peter and Rose Kowalski went a short time later to Managua.

Father Heinzen returned to Nicaragua in December 1988, spent time in Managua, and then used his skills in aiding in the Bluefields reconstruction following the Hurricane Joan devastation which struck October 22, 1988. March 1, 1989, he was allowed to return to Waspam.

3. Rufus Manuel Calderon was the full name of the Sandinista commander of Northeast Nicaragua.

"All Indians Were Contras"

1. The same day of the initial executions at Leimus, the Sandinistas bombed Aasang and San Carlos, killing sixty Indians with a number of eighty-pound bombs. Many other atrocities were inflicted upon the Indians in the Coco River sector of Nicaragua.

U.S. Department of State, *Human Rights in Nicaragua Under the Sandinistas,* 184-189.
Cf. Belli, *Breaking Faith,* 110.
Cf. Edmund W. and Julia Robb, op. cit., 139-140.

Archibald Theofilo

"Great Economic Strides"

1. The meaning of the word "Creole," as used by Archibald Theofilo and given earlier in the footnotes, is defined by *The American Heritage Dictionary of the English Language,* William Morris, editor, Boston: American Heritage Publishing Co., Inc., and Houghton Mifflin Company, 1973 on p. 312—"...A person of Negro descent born in the Western Hemisphere, as distinguished from a Negro brought from Africa. Also called 'Creole Negro.'"

First to Protest

1. It is interesting to note how effective the Sandinista propaganda works in American news media. Cf. *Facts on File* (Fri., Oct. 17, 1980), 792-F1. The statement is made that twenty people were arrested among the five hundred persons protesting.

2. Bill Kenkelen, "Cubans criticizing religion," *National Catholic Reporter,* Fri., Feb. 22, 1980, 26—"…[Archbishop] Obando said some Cubans currently teaching in Nicaragua 'have been ridiculing the religious beliefs of the people.'"

Cf. Dozier, op. cit., 235—"A social anthropologist who made a postrevolution study of government-Indian relations in the Atlantic region in 1980 notes that the first Sandinista fighters to enter Mosquita were profoundly baffled by what they found: an apathetic if not openly hostile population who refused to understand that they were the victims of imperialism or that General Sandino was a heroic figure." After a year of what he characterizes as "notable achievements," "…serious cultural animosities persist and continue to evolve in the revolutionary context. A general mistrust or, at best, apathy vis-á-vis the revolution prevails." (See Philippe Bourgois, "Class, Ethnicity, and the State Among the Miskito Amerindians of Northeastern Nicaragua," *Latin American Perspective* 8, Riverside, Calif.: Latin American Perspectives, Inc., Spring 1981), 26, 32.

Cf. "Marxism and Christianity in Revolutionary Central America," *Hearings before the Subcommittee on Security and Terrorism of the Committee in the Judiciary of the United States Senate* (Washington, D.C., Oct. 18-19, 1983), 137—Wycliffe Diego said, "I think the civil war going on in Nicaragua right now is as much religious as it is political because most of the people that are joining the rebel forces are saying that their primary reason for doing so is the religious persecution and the anti-religious stance of the FSLN."

Pressure and Escape

1. This person, Marcelo Martinos, was forced to flee Nicaragua and is now in the United States.

2. "Dory" is the name for a dugout canoe on the Mosquito Coast of Central America.

3. Shortly after this interview, telephone contact was made with his son, who told Archibald that he had just been released from jail.

East Coast Soviet Base

1. At Rus Rus, Honduras, southwest of Mocoron along the Rus Rus River and near the Coco River, a very large meeting was held on June 12-16, 1987. Represented were all of the Freedom Fighter groups from the eastern coast of Nicaragua who were fighting Sandinista Communism. Leaders worked to iron out differences and to present a united front. An umbrella

organization for the four thousand East Coast Freedom Fighters was formed and given the title YATAMA, which meant "United Indian Nations of the Motherland." This included KISAN, MISURASATA, MISURA, and SICC.

SICC stands for "Southern Indigenous Creole Community." Following the meeting at Rus Rus, the Creoles were in the process of reorganizing this group.

2. However, because of all the turmoil and terror caused by the Sandinistas in the first half of the '80s, in the second half some concessions were forced upon them and Zelaya was divided into two autonomous regions.

3. Cf. U.S. Department of State, *Human Rights in Nicaragua Under the Sandinistas*, 190-193—"Indian Nations and the Nicaraguan State" by Bernard Nietschmann.

Cf. Richard J. Meislin, "Sandinistas Reach Pact With Indians," *New York Times*, Tues., April 23, 1985, L-A8.

4. Cf. Shirley Christian, "Miskito Says U.S. Blocks Unity," *New York Times*, Tues., Oct. 8, 1985, L-A4.

Ruth Lissa Gasden de Castillo

"Mommy, Mommy! Sandinista Coming"

1. A former British colony (British Honduras) in Central America bordering Guatemala's northeast region.

"Refugees Are Contras and Are Nobody!"

1. *Cazaba* is Spanish for cassava. *Webster's Ninth New Collegiate Dictionary* (Springfield, Mass.: G.& C. Merriam Co., 1983), 212—Cassava is "...any of several plants (genus *Manihot*) of the spurge family grown in the tropics for their fleshy edible root stocks which yield a nutritious starch...."

"Contras Have Prayer Every Morning"

1. Cf. "Human Rights in Nicaragua," *United States Senate Hearings before the Sub Committee on Western Hemisphere Affairs*, 13-14. Eliot Abrams, the Assistant Secretary of Inter-American Affairs, said that Moravian leadership excused the Sandinista government. These leaders claimed that the Sandinistas had a legitimate security reason for doing what they did where the Miskitos were, but Abrams was blunt in refuting this by saying that this type of reasoning "...just doesn't wash."

The Moravian Church in the United States has about sixty thousand members. It has not been much of a problem for the Sandinistas to make their influence felt with them. Cf. "U.S. Criticized on Nicaragua," *New York Times,* Sat., Aug. 13, 1983, L-A3.

2. On January 13, 1988, a letter was posted to the the Rev. Avery Post, President of the United Church of Christ in New York City, along with a press release copy from the Nicaraguan Resistance. Copies of this letter were sent to Jim Wright, the Speaker of the United States House of Representatives, and to the United States news media. The letter was signed by a deacon, Stanley A. Patrick, Jr., of the Salem United Church of Christ, New Orleans, Louisiana, and in part stated, "You and the church leadership of the Office For Church in Society as well as other main stream church hierarchies always headline data you receive from your friends, the Sandinistas, concerning unproven humanitarian atrocities by the Contras...."

"Copies of this information are being sent to the media and Speaker Jim Wright...sadly like you, they too embrace the atheistic regime of Sandinista communists."

The press release detailed the capture of two women Freedom Fighters, Maria Bastamante Aguirre (Comando Zoila) and Aureliana Carrasco Benavides (Comando nineteen and twenty years old respectively. They had been fighting on the Northern Front at Las Piedras near the town of Pantasma in the Department of Jinotega. On November 30, 1987, after running out of ammunition, these young girls were captured by the EPS, the Popular Sandinista Army, stripped of clothing, tied to a tree, raped with continued torture, and finally decapitated.

The victims were given a proper burial by local people, who also informed local Freedom Fighter patrols in the area. The Nicaraguan Resistance reported this to international human rights organizations and the National Reconciliation Commission in charge of the Esquipulas II Accords which were a part of the Central American Peace Plan endorsed earlier in 1987 by leaders of Central America nations.

Afterword

1. Cf. *Report of the Caribbean Commission Investigative Team,* op. cit.—on page 42 of the report is an article called "Persecution of the Religious by the Sandinistas," by Dr. Alton Ochsner, Chairman of the Caribbean Commission. He states, "The Caribbean Commission has documented more than five hundred incidences where the Sandinistas have severely persecuted the Religious who refuse to cooperate with them. This registry continues to grow.... The reports are the result of interviews with Nicaraguan clergy and some civilians, with refugees and wounded Freedom Fighters that I have attended. They are based on personal experience or visual accounts.

"The U.S. public is unaware of the extent of Religious Persecution by the Sandinistas because the News Media ignores it. The Caribbean Commission has been unsuccessful in getting any of the Media to publicize the findings of its Investigative work in Nicaragua. The few atrocities against the Religious that I have seen reported in the News recently have been blamed on the 'Contras.' These reports come from the Sandinistas the Caribbean Commission Investigative Team could not find any Nicaraguans not associated with the Sandinistas that could verify them."

2. Leiken and Ruben, op. cit., 235—FSLN anthem trans. by Gladys Segal.

3. Cf. John Moody, "Lights Out In Nicaragua," *Time*, Mon., Feb. 29, 1988, 55.

Cf. John Silber, "How A Country Goes Communist to Stay," *National Review*, Fri., March 4, 1988, 18-19.

4. Cf. Gerald M. Boyd, "Reagan Says Nicaragua Runs a Campaign of Lies," *New York Times*, Thurs., Feb. 20, 1986, L-A6.

5. This title was quoted on the book jacket of op. cit., Somoza (as to told to Jack Cox). Originally, this quote was from an article in the 1980 "Scoreboard Edition of American Opinion Magazine."

6. Larry Martz, "Next Target: Nicaragua." *Newsweek*, Mon., Nov. 14, 1983, 44.

Cf. *Taking the Stand*, 571. Lieutenant Colonel North said, "…American people have not been given all of the information…very difficult thing to get out the straight story on the Nicaraguan resistance, and the true perversion of the revolution, undertaken by the Sandinistas. Their propaganda machine is very, very effective."

Cf. "Nicaragua now taking harder line," *St. Paul Pioneer Press Dispatch*, Mon., May 16, 1988, 3A— "Apparently convinced that the Contra guerrilla army is collapsing, the Sandinista government is taking a new and harder line against opposition groups in the country."

7. Cf. Martin Tolchin, "Reports of Anti-Sandinista Aid Worry Senators," *New York Times*, Wed., April 6, 1983, L-A8.

Cf. "House rejects aid to contras," *Star Tribune*, Minneapolis, Minn., Thurs., Feb. 4, 1988, 1A. The House of Representatives Democratic majority defeated the President's bid to support the Freedom Fighters with arms and humanitarian aid by a vote of 219-211 on February 3, 1988.

Cf. "Senate endorses Reagan's contra-aid plan in symbolic vote," *Star Tribune*, Minneapolis, Minn., Fri., Feb. 5, 1988, 1. The Senate voted 51-48 to support the President's plan.

Cf. Cal Thomas, op. cit. "Congress, others ignore lessons of all communists' barbarism," *St. Paul Pioneer Press Dispatch*, Mon., March 28, 1988, 15A.

Cf. David Hess, "Democrats Propose Contra-Aid Plan, But Dole Isn't Satisfied," *St. Paul Pioneer Press Dispatch*, Thurs., Aug. 4, 1988, p.18A.

8. Cf. Daniel 6:1-15.

Bibliography

Interviews

Nery Daniel Colindres, Milba Colindres de Rayo, Carlos Humberto Hernandez, Rasario Aguilar de Sevilla, Jesus Sandoval, Theofilo Orozco Flores, Ray Hudson, Jose Ramon Gonzales Rameriz, Jose Ines Aguilar Rodriguez, Dani Lewis, Agenor Rodriguez Carcino, Maura Carbajal, Dr. Carlos Rodolfo Icaza Espinosa, "Martin," "Patricio," Zaida Rodriguez vda de Ortez, Bayardo Antonio Santeliz, Col. Abraham Garcia Turcios, Lindberg Mueller, Dr. Marco Antonio Manzanares, Jose "Capi" Jackson, Otis Fredrick, Transito Lacayo, Frank and Tere McEwan Bendana, Daisy Montiel Rodriguez, Manuel Jiron, Joraila Wallace, Edwin Muller, "Truksulu," Charley and Eunice Hooker Sang, Carlos Muller Schrader, Father Hugh Heinzen, Julio Equiguren, Salvador Montenegro, Archibald Theofilo, Pastor Ricardo Duarte, Joaquin Navas, Ruth Lissa Gasden de Castillo, John Baldwin, Diego Lacayo Oyanguren, Dr. Alexander Bolanos, Brother Julius Winkler, Dr. Bernard Nietschmann, Douglas Payne, Nana Gill, Russell Stendal, and Bill Stewart.

Books:

Bell, Belden, ed. *Nicaragua: An Ally Under Siege.* Washington, D.C.: Council on American Affairs, 1978.

Belli, Humberto. *Breaking Faith.* Westchester, Ill.: Crossway Books, 1985.

Belli, Humberto. *Nicaragua—Christians Under Fire.* Garden City, Mich.: Puebla Institute, 1984.

Booth, John A. *The End and the Beginning: The Nicaraguan Revolution.* Boulder, Colorado: Westview Press, 1985.

Buckley, William F. *Right Reason.* Garden City, New York: Doubleday and Company, Inc., 1985.

Christian, Shirley. *Nicaragua: Revolution in the Family.* New York: Vintage Books, 1986.

Denton, Jeremiah A. *When Hell Was in Session.* Lake Wylie, S.C.: Reprinted by Robert E. Hopper & Associates, 1982 Jeremiah Denton Associates Inc.

Dickey, Christopher. *With the Contras.* New York: Touchstone-Simon and Schuster, 1987.

Diederich, Bernard. *Somoza and the Legacy of U.S. Involvement in Central America.* New York: E. Dutton, 1980.

Dox, Ida. *Melloni's Illustrated Medical Dictionary* (2d ed.). Baltimore: Williams and Wilkins, 1985.

Dozier, Craig L. *Nicaragua's Mosquito Shore: The Years of British and American Presence.* University of Alabama: The University of Alabama Press, 1985.

Fiere, Paulo. *Pedagogy of the Oppressed.* Trans. by Myra Bergman Ramos. New York: Herder & Herder, 1970.

Frangui, Carlos. *Family Portrait with Fidel.* Trans. from Spanish by Alfred MacAdam. New York: Random House, 1984.

Goodman, Walter. *The Committee.* New York: Farrar, Straus & Giroux, 1986.

Hargis, Billy James. *Forewarned.* Tulsa, Okla.: Christian Crusade Books, 1988.

Harris, Richard L., and Vilas, Carlos M. (eds.). *Nicaragua: A Revolution Under Siege.* London: Zed Books, Ltd., 1985.

Hoover, J. Edgar. *Masters of Deceit.* New York: Holt, Rinehart & Winston, 1958.

Hugh, Thomas. *The Cuban Revolution.* New York: Harper and Row, 1977.

Jiron, Manuel. *Quien es Quien en Nicaragua.* San Jose, Costa Rica: Editoral Radio Amor, 1986.

Leiken, Robert S., and Rubin, Barry, eds. *The Central American Crises Reader.* New York: Summit Books, 1987.

Macheivelli, Niccolo. *The Prince.* New York: Mentor, 1952.

Martin, Malachi. *The Jesuits.* New York: The Linden Press—Simon & Schuster, Inc., 1987.

Meyer, Harvey K. *Historical Dictionary of Nicaragua* (Latin American Historical Dictionaries #6). Metuchen, N.J.: The Scarecrow Press, Inc., 1972.

Miller, Valerie. *Between Struggle and Hope—The Nicaraguan Literacy Crusade.* Boulder and London: Westview Press, 1985.

Murray, William J. *Nicaragua: Portrait of a Tragedy.* Toronto: Mainroads Productions, Inc., 1987.

Nixon, Richard. *The Real War.* New York: Warner Books, 1980.

North, Oliver L. *Taking the Stand.* New York: Pocket Books, 1987.

Nuccio, Richard A. *Who's Wrong Who's Right in Central America.* New York: Facts On File Publications, 1986.

Robb, Edmund W. and Julia. *The Betrayal of the Church.* Westchester, Ill.: Crossway Books, 1986.

Rosset, Peter, and Vandermeer, John (eds.). *Nicaragua: Unfinished Revolution.* New York: Grove Press, In., 1986.

Rushdie, Salman. *The Jaguar Smile.* New York: Penguin Books-Viking Penguin, Inc., 1988.

Stendal, Russell. *Rescue the Captors.* 3rd ed. Burnsville, Minn.: Ransom Press International, 1984.

Somoza, Anastasio (as told to Jack Cox). *Nicaragua Betrayed.* Belmont, Mass.: Western Islands, 1980.

The Holy Bible. Revised Standard Version. New York: A.J. Holmen Company, 1971.

Villadares, Armando (trans. Andrew Hurley). *Against All Hope.* New York: Alfred A. Knopf, 1986.

Webster's New Collegiate Dictionary. Springfield, Mass.: G. & C. Merriam Co., 1976.

Zwerling, Philip, and Martin, Connie. *Nicaragua: A New Kind of Revolution.* Westport, Conn.: Lawrence Hill & Company, 1985.

Articles, Documents, Map, Video, and Miscellaneous:

"Aleksandr Solzhenitsyn." *Congressional Record,* 128:1, Jan. 28, 1982, 396-400.

Anderson, David E. "U.S. Church Support For Sandinistas Hit." *Washington Post,* July 14, 1984, G10.

Antoine, Charles. "Scénario et objectif de l'affaire Pellecer." *Etudes,* Péres de Compagnie de la Jésus, Paris, France, Jan. 1982, 732.

Askin, Steve. "Detained Jesuit Visits Washington." *National Catholic Reporter,* Kansas City, Mo., Dec. 31, 1982. 2.

Bennett, Susan. "Bush changes course with contras." *St. Paul Pioneer Press Dispatch,* March 25, 1989, 3A.

Blum, Lenore. "The Literary Campaign, Nicaragua Style." *Caribbean Review,* Winter 1981.

"Bohemia" and "Bohemian Brethren," vol. 3, and "Moravian Church," vol. 16. *Universal Standard Encyclopedia.* New York: Standard Reference Works Publishing House, Inc., 1958.

Borrell, John. "Nicaragua: At War With Itself." *Time,* Nov. 16, 1987, 41-42.

Bourdreau, Richard. "Economic Woes Nicaragua's Top Problem." *Star Tribune,* Minneapolis, Minn., Nov. 27, 1987, A24.

Boyd, Gerald M. "Reagan Says Nicaragua Runs a Campaign of Lies." *New York Times,* Feb. 20, 1986, L-A6.

Callahan, William R., and Pomerleau, Dolores C. "'Irresponsible' Words Polarize Nicaragua." *National Catholic Reporter,* Kansas City, Mo., March 25, 1983, 7.

"Cardinal Obando: The Church in Nicaragua Is Persecuted (trans)." *La Prensa,* Tegucigalpa, Honduras, May 10, 1986.

Caribbean Commission Investigative Team. "The Tragedy of Nicaragua." New Orleans: *The Caribbean Commission,* 1987.

Christian, Shirley, "Miskito Says U.S. Blocks Unity." *New York Times,* Oct. 8, 1985, L-A4.

"Contras call for new aid after talks collapse." *Star Tribune,* Minneapolis, Minn., June 11, 1988, 3A.

Day, Mark R. "Interruption during homily 'unplanned', observers say." *National Catholic Reporter,* Kansas City, Mo., March 25, 1983, 7.

Daremblum, Jaime. "Costa Rica Responds to the Enemy Within." *Wall Street Journal,* June 14, 1985, 25.

Dicky, Christopher. "Managua Literacy Drive: Too Political?" *Washington Post,* May 24, 1980, A11.

"8 Killed In Nicaragua In Separatist Revolt." (Reuters) *Washington Post,* Feb. 24, 1981, A8.

Directory of Associations in Canada. Toronto: Micromedia, Limited, 1987, 8th ed.

"Duarte to Seek More U.S. Aid." *New York Times,* Sept. 12, 1986, I12.

Echegaray, Max. "Central America 'Backfire': Juntas quote Pope, attack Jesuits— Jesuits' political, social involvement challenged." *National Catholic Reporter,* Kansas City, Mo., Feb. 8, 1980, 3, 8.

Encyclopedia of Associations. Vol. 4, *International Organizations.* 21st ed. Detroit: Gale Research, 1987.

Errickson, Kurt. "Warfare Uproots Nicaraguan Indians." *Minnesota Daily,* University of Minnesota, Nov. 11, 1986, 1.

Epstein, Jack, and Evans, J. H. "Indians, Sandinistas vie for control in Nicaragua." *National Catholic Reporter,* Kansas City, Mo., Oct. 22, 1982, 1, 7.

"Ex-guardsmen given pardons by Nicaragua." *St. Paul Pioneer Press Dispatch,* March 18, 1989, 6A.

"Central America" in *Facts On File.* New York: Facts On File, Inc. Sept. 25, 1987, 687.

"Nicaragua," in *Facts On File.* New York: Facts On File, Inc. Oct. 17, 1980, 792.

"Paraguay Breaks Relations," in *Facts On File.* New York: Facts On File, Inc. Oct. 17, 1980, 792.

"Fr. Pellecer's Testimony." *The Wanderer.* St. Paul, Aug. 23, 1984, 5.

"Oliver North Fight for Freedom." 1987 American Freedom Coalition, Washington, D.C. Videocassette produced by Global Image Assoc. Inc., Washington, D.C. Directed. by Vince Clews and Assoc., Inc. Approx. 60 min. Made in U.S.A.

Gadea, Fredy, and Centeno, Armando, "Propuesta De Ayuda Humanitaria." *En Algun Lugan de Nicaragua: El Comando Regional Quilali, Resistencia Nicaraguense,* Abril 26, 1988, 9.

Gerth, Jeff. "On The Trail of Latin Mystery, C.I.A. Footprints." *New York Times,* Oct. 6, 1983, 1, 12.

Hall, Carla. "The Music and Message of Nicaragua." *Washington Post,* May 8, 1980, C7.

Harris, Art. "The Sandinistas' Sister-in-Arms." *Washington Post,* Oct. 4, 1984, B1.

Hess, David. "Democrats Propose Contra-Aid Plan, But Dole Isn't Satisfied." *St. Paul Pioneer Press Dispatch,* Aug. 4, 1988, 18A.

"House rejects aid to contras." *Star Tribune*, Minneapolis, Minn., Feb. 4, 1988, 1.

"How to Handle Nicaragua." *Newsweek*, April 29, 1985, 38.

"Human Rights in Nicaragua." United States Senate Hearings before Sub-Committee on Western Hemisphere Affairs of the Committee on Foreign Relations, Washington, D.C., Feb. 25 and March 1, 1982.

"Immigration Rules Are Eased For Nicaraguan Exiles In U.S." *New York Times*, July 9, 1987, L-A8.

"In These Last Days More Than 50 Hondurans Have Died Because of the 'Nica' Military Situation (trans)." *El Hearldo*, Tegucigalpa, Honduras, Mayo 3, 1986.

"Iran-Contra Affair." Report of Select House Committee to Investigate Covert Arms Transactions with Iran and Senate Committee on Secret Military Assistance to Iran and the Nicaraguan Opposition Section II, The Minority Report. Washington, D.C., 1987.

"Iran-Contra Investigation," Joint Hearings Before the Select Committee on Secret Military Assistance to Iran and the Nicaraguan Opposition and the House Select Committee to Investigate Covert Arms Transaction With Iran—Testimony of Richard V. Secord, May 5 through May 8, 1987, Washington, D.C.: U.S. Government Printing Office, 1988.

Kenkelen, Bill. "Cubans criticizing religion." *National Catholic Reporter*, Kansas City, Mo., Feb. 22, 1980, 26.

Kinzer, Stephen. "Nicaragua Denies Its Troops Invaded Honduras." *New York Times*, March 26, 1986, L-A6.

Kinzer, Stephen. "Nicaragua Men Fleeing Draft Fill Honduran Refugee Camp." *New York Times*, April 11, 1985, A1.

Kinzer, Stephen. "Nicaraguan Indians Began to Return." *New York Times*, July 27, 1985, L-A1.

Kinzer, Stephen, " The Way Home Is Hard For Indians of Nicaragua." *New York Times*, Aug. 22, 1985, L-A2.

Koeppel, Barbara. "Nicaragua Sending All of Its Citizens to School." *Christian Science Monitor*, Jan.17, 1980, 5.

"La Prensa Is Crusading Critic of Nicaragua Regime." *Star Tribune*, Minneapolis,March 13, 1988, 23A.

La Tribuna, Tegucigalpa, Honduras, Marzo 31, 1986 (contains an article on Honduran citizens fleeing from border areas).

Le Moyne, James. "U.S. Copters Reported Ready to Ferry Troops to the Border Area." *New York Times,* March 26, 1986, L-A1.

Magnotta, Vince and Ann. "Costa Rica's Literacy Boom." *Christian Science Monitor,* Nov. 1, 1985, 31.

Maraniss, David. "In the Valley: The Sanctuary House." *Washington Post,* Nov. 20, 1985, A1.

Martz, Larry. "Next Target: Nicaragua." *Newsweek,* Nov. 14, 1983, 44.

"Marxism and Christianity in Revolutionary Central America." Hearings before the Subcommittee on Security and Terrorism of the Committee on the Judiciary of the United States Senate, Washington, D.C., Oct. 18 and 19, 1983, 164-258.

McCartney, Robert J. "Waiting in Honduras: Nicaraguans Fleeing War and Draft Form Support Base for Guerrillas." *Washington Post,* Sept. 6, 1985, A1.

McNeil-Lehrer program, National Public Television, KTCA, Minneapolis-St. Paul, Minn., June 15, 1988.

Meislin, Richard J. "Sandinistas Reach Pact With Indians." *New York Times,* April 23, 1985, L-A8.

Moody, John. "Lights Out in Managua." *Time,* Feb. 29, 1988, 55.

Mott, Gordon. "In Nicaragua, the Lucky Buy Plenty With Dollars." *New York Times,* Nov. 12, 1984, L-A8.

"Nicaragua expels U.S. envoy, cites 'state terrorism.'" *Star Tribune,* Minneapolis, Minn., July 12, 1988, 1A.

"Nicaragua: Rebels Killed U.S. Born Bishop." *Star Tribune,* Minneapolis, Minn., Dec. 22, 1983, A14.

Nicaraguan Biogragphies: A Resource Book. Special Report No. 174, United States Department of State, Bureau of Public Affairs, Washington, D.C., Jan. 1988.

"Nicaraguan Prisoners Denounce Harassments—They are chained inside damp places. They are confined in large numbers to unventilated cells. They are subjected to make belief executions (trans.)." *La Tribuna,* Tegucigalpa, Honduras,Noviembre 5, 1986, 47

"Nicaragua to allow 10 priests to return, news show to resume." *Star Tribune,* Minneapolis, Minn., March 16, 1989, 20A.

Nietschmann, Bernard. Sumo Miskito, and Rama Nations—Map. University of California, Berkeley, Department of Geography, July 1985.

Novak, Michael. "Illusions About Nicaragua." *National Review,* June 29, 1984, 38.

Nusser, Nancy. "Nicaragua's uprooted Indians." *Christian Science Monitor,* July 26, 1985, 16.

Ohland, Klaudine, and Schneider, Robin (eds.). "National Revolution and Indigenous Identity: The Conflict between Sandinist[a]s and Miskito Indians on Nicaragua's Atlantic Coast." IWGIA Document No. 47. Copenhagen: International Work Group for Indigenous Affairs, Nov. 1983.

"Ortega announces austerity plan for Nicaragua." *Star Tribune,* Minneapolis, Minn., Jan. 31, 1989, 1A.

"Ortega gives U.N. plan to repatriate contra rebels." *Star Tribune,* Minneapolis, Minn., April 19, 1989, 16A.

"Ortega says contra war is over, offers peace effort." *Star Tribune,* Minneapolis, Minn., Feb. 2, 1989, 11A.

"Other News." *Star Tribune,* Minneapolis, Minn. March 18, 1989, 3A.

Payne, Douglas W. "The Democratic Mask—The Consolidation of the Sandinista Revolution." *Perspectives On Freedom* 3. New York: Freedom House, 1985, 20, 24.

Pellecer, Luis Eduardo Faena (SJ). *Conferencia de Prensa.* (videocassette) St. Charles, Mo.: Nicaraguan Information Center, May 3, 1981.

"Prelate Carballo: Sandinistas Intensify Repression (trans), *La Prensa,* Tegucigalpa, Honduras, Mayo 3, 1986.

"Priest Assesses Nicaraguan Tribes' Lot." *New York Times,* Jan. 3, 1984, A15.

Radosh, Ronald. "Nicaragua Revisited." *New Republic,* Aug. 3, 1987. 22.

"Reagan's Night For Refugees—At The Fund Raising Dinner, Voice From Nicaragua." *Washington Post,* April 16, 1985, C1.

"Rebel Planes Strafe Nica Airfield." *Star Tribune,* Minneapolis, Minn., Sept. 9, 1983, A13.

"Record of World Events." *Keesing's Contemporary Archives.* London: Keesing's Publications (Longman Group Ltd.), 1980 (30317-18) & 1981 (30660).

"Rightist win by a landslide in El Salvador legislative vote." *St. Paul Pioneer Press Dispatch,* March 22, 1988, 4A.

Roberts, Steven V. "Lawmakers Say Raid Will Help Cause Of Contras." *New York Times,* March 26, 1986, L-A6.

Roche, Joe. "Sandinista Repressing Church in Nicaragua." *Minnesota Daily,* Oct. 23, 1987, 7.

Ross, Jim. "Nicaragua convoy, stopped at border, back in Minnesota." *St. Paul Pioneer Press Dispatch,* July 21, 1988, 1B.

Russell, George. "Nothing Will Stop This Revolution" (reported by Timothy Loughrans, William McWhirter, Alessandra Stanley). *Time,* Oct. 17, 1983, 37.

"Sandinista—Contra Talks in Stalemate: Holiday Truce Unlikely, Cardinal says." *Star Tribune,* Minneapolis, Minn., Dec. 5, 1987, 3A.

Saxon, Wolfgang. "Nora Astorga, Sandinista Hero and Delegate to U.N., Dies at 39." *New York Times,* Feb. 15, 1988, 20.

"Sects Under Attack In Nicaragua." *New York Times,* Aug. 12, 1982, L-A3.

"Senate endorses Reagan's contra-aid plan in symbolic vote." *Star Tribune,* Minneapolis, Minn., Feb. 5, 1988, 1.

Serafino, Nina. *Contra Aid: 1981-March 1987—Summary and Chronology of Major Congressional Action on Key Legislation Concerning U.S. Aid to the Anti-Sandinista Guerrillas.* Congressional Research Service. Washington, D.C.: Library of Congress, July 21, 1987.

Silber, John. "How A Country Goes Communist to Stay." *National Review,* March 4, 1988, 18-19.

Simons, Marlise. "Pope Insists Priests Quit Sandinista Posts Or He Will Not Visit." *New York Times,* Dec. 3, 1982, L-A1.

"Situacion de Refugiados en Honduras," Office of the United Nations High Commissioner for Refugees, Tegucigalpa, Honduras: 1 de Mayo de 1986, 1 de Septiembre de 1986, 1 de Noviembre de 1986, 1 de Octubre de 1987.

Szamuely. George. "Rushdie May Appreciate Democracy Better Now." *Wall Street Journal,* Feb. 22, 1989, A14.

Taubman, Philip. "U.S. Says It Halted Talks With Nicaragua—Four Nicaraguan Priests Suspended." *New York Times,* Jan. 19, 1985, L-A4.

The American Heritage Dictionary of the English Language. Boston: American Heritage Publishing Co., Inc., and Houghton Mifflin Company, 1973, 312.

"The Majority Of Nicaraguans Resist Marxism: Obando (trans)." *La Prensa,* Tegucigalpa, Honduras, Mayo 13, 1986.

The Tragedy Of Nicaragua. New Orleans, La.: The Caribbean Commission, 1987.

Thomas, Cal. "Congress, others ignore lessons of all communists' barbarism." *St. Paul Pioneer Press Dispatch,* March 28, 1988, 15A.

Tolchin, Martin. "Reports of Anti-Sandinista Aid Worry Senators." *New York Times,* April 6, 1983, A9.

Treumann, Beverly. "Chronicle of the Crusade (1)—Nicaragua's Second Revolution." *Christianity and Crises,* Nov. 2, 1981, 298.

Uhlig, Mark A. "Somoza's Soldiers Rejoining a Society Divided on Pardon." *New York Times,* March 17, 1989, 4Y.

"U.S. Criticized On Nicaragua." *New York Times,* Aug. 13, 1983, L-A3.

U.S. Department of State and Department of Defense. *The Challenge to Democracy in Central America.* Washington, D.C., June 1986.

U.S. Department of State. *Dispossessed—The Miskito Indians in Sandinista Nicaragua.* Washington, D.C., June 1986.

U.S. Department of State. *Human Rights in Nicaragua Under the Sandinistas—From Revolution to Repression.* Washington, D.C., Dec. 1986.

"Vatican Criticizes Office-Holding Nicaraguan Priests." *The Wanderer,* St. Paul, Aug. 23, 1984, 1, 7.

Volsky, George. "Group Would Aid Nicaraguans Here." *New York Times,* Aug. 8, 1985, A11.

Wines, Michael, and Doyle McManus. "Contra-White House Meeting reflected fading hopes of victory." *Star Tribune,* Minneapolis, Minn., March 25, 1988, A1.

Weintraub, Bernard. "Reagan Urges Arms Aid For Nicaraguan Rebels." *New York Times,* Dec. 15, 1985, L-A1.

"World of Religion." *Washington Post,* Oct. 20, 1984, C10.

Yearbook of International Organizations. Vols. 1-3. New York: K. G. Saur, Publisher, 1986-87.

Index

To order additional copies of this book,
please send full amount plus $5.00 for
postage and handling for the first book and
$1.00 for each additional book.
Minnesota residents add 7.125 percent sales tax

Send orders to:

Galde Press
PO Box 460
Lakeville, Minnesota 55044-0460

Credit card orders call 1–800–777–3454
Fax (952) 891–6091
Visit our website at *www.galdepress.com*
and download our free catalog,
or write for our catalog.